The Half-Way Tree

The Half-Way Tree

poems selected and new

1970-2000

John B. Lee

Black Moss Press
2001

Published by Black Moss Press at 2450 Byng Road, 2450 Byng Road, Windsor, Ontario, N8W3E8. Black Moss books are distributed in Canada and the U.S. by Firefly Books, 3680 Victoria Park Ave., Willowdale, Ontario, Canada. All orders should be directed there.

Black Moss would like to acknowledge the support of the Canada Council for the Arts and the Ontario Arts Council for its publishing program.

National Library of Canada Cataloguing in Publication Data

Lee, John B., 1951-
        The halfway tree

Poems.
ISBN 0-88753-354-X

        I. Title.

PS8573.E348H34 2001   C811'.54   C2001-901862-2
PR9199.3.L39H34 2001

Acknowledgements

New poems from The Half-Way Tree have appeared in Aethlon, The Amethyst Review, The Antigonish Review, Arc 2000, Bad News Bingo, Convergence: Poets for Peace, Diverse City Too, Diverse City 2000, Backwater Review, Carousel, Celebrate the Thames, Cider Press Review, Cranberry Tree Press Anthology, CVII, Dandelion, Descant, Doors of Morning, The Fiddlehead, Following the Plough, Grain, HEArt Quarterly, Henry's Creature, I Want to Be the Poet of Your Kneecaps, Kairos, Larger than Life, Literary Gourmet, Literary Pages, Losers First, The Malahat Review, Map of Austin, Mentor's Cannon, New People: The Peach and Social Justice Newspaper of Pittsburg, 90 Poets of the Nineties, No Love Lost, Open Windows, Open Windows II, Open Windows III, Outreach, Paper Tiger, People's Poetry Newsletter, Poem Cards, Poem Cards Anthology, Poets for Peace Flyer and web site, Prairie Fire, Prism International, The Night of My Conception, Scene, Seeds Anthology, Sing for the Inner Ear, Smaller than God, Snapping Turtle & Rattler, Souwesto Words CD, Visionary Tradition, Waiting for You to Speak, Whiplash Poetry Festival Anthology, Zygote, Windsor Review and been broadcast on the year end television special "Canadian Heroes."

in addition to the award-winning poems from the selected work, the new poems have been honoured as follows:

"One Scorched Glove On a Beach" won first place in the 1998 People's Poem Award

"The Night My Brain Froze Four Inches Back" was Editor's Choice in Zygote Magazine

"No Such Place as Nowhere" was named runner-up in Carousel Magazine's poetry award

"Thinking Like Children" and *"The Knights of Columbus Lobster Fest, Ancaster"* received an Honourable Mention in This Magazine's Great Canadian Literary Hunt, 1998

"The Two Chicagos" received sole Honourable mention in HEArt Quarterly and received a nomination for the Pushcart Prize 1999

"The Half-Way Tree" "The Red Sweater and the Myth of Sunday" "The Boy Who Ate Flies" "The Night the Simpson Barn Almost Fell" and *"My Cousin Fell in Love with Archie"* received the distinction of Editor's Choice in the Open Window Award

"I'll Miss Your Soups" received Honourable mention as Editor's Choice in the *No Love Lost* anthology

"The Knights of Columbus Lobster Fest, Ancaster" won first place in Cranberry Tree Press's poetry competition 2000

"The Ghost of Erwin Rommel" placed in the top five of the winter 1999 People's Poetry Poem Awards

"The Dog Who Died in the Dark" won Honourable mention in the 2000 Sandburg/Livesay awards

"Thinking Like Children" won second place in the Canadian Poetry Association's poetry awards 2000

"Walking Along Lake Erie" won the Lexikon poetry award 2000

Several of the poems from the manuscript were short-listed for the 1999 Canadian Literary Awards

No Such Place As Nowhere

I was born on a farm
on a hill near Highgate
named for Highgate, England.
Every spring the west muck would flood
and our farm become an island.
My uncle made a raft
and I sailed the shallow sea
from lane to fence going shore to shore
across the wool of waves
like Odysseus
returning from the war
lashed to the belly of a sheep.
And I lived
among seven humans
in a large brick house
behind a stand of pine
a palisade against the distant road
each low dead branch
bristled like a broken comb.
And I feared the wicked wells in the yard
one deep in the earth where troll rivers ran
one shallow as a dragon gullet.
And I suffered the sense that we were culled
and set aside
and far from all adventure
though passing trains belched fires
that caught the fields
and left us beating smoke
beneath a lonely elm.
And in the winter
when the snows came
angeling down from a house-cleaned heaven
and the ground cured like drying lime
so it was set and frozen
with manure puddles hard as English toffee
and the marbled candy
of clay and windy water blown together

beside small ponds
like the window panes of abandoned houses
lane on the earth by thieves.
And I've never seemed so locked
since then
since the rusty hasp of my soul
broke free
chasing what I remember
from my verandah cave
where I sat and surveyed the world
going cat death by cat death
until I became a man
too large to stay.

No Such Place as Nowhere

Appropriated Voice

I am many voices
not my own. I will not be
bruised into silence
like October apples
gone ripe-heavy
winding once before they fall
to cider
and a drunken retreat of worms.
I will sing
inside the withered core
as a seed
that holds the tree.
I will sing
as the climbing boy
where he bends the bough warping after fruit.
I will sing
as bees in blooms
buzzing my golden kazoo
in a skiffle band of hives.
I will sing
with his honey-scented head
my veined wings humming
like a hurry-up angel.
I will sing
as the birds of spring.
I will sing
as the birds of winter.
I will sing
as rain sings
going by deep-down drum booms
of far off thunder
across your houses
coming close and climbing
to the wind-drunk orchard
cracking half the crop of summer

with the random pruning
of my song of storms.
And I will come
softly tapping
like a lost blindness
searching its way through the field
hushing the edge of everything
it touches even to where
the damp grass yields
worshipping the wet weight
of my having arrived

I raise my voice
announcing who I am
within this mask of song.

The Train Wreck

Where the train cars
were lying
you could hear the pigs screaming.
Some of them were running loose
their sides torn
trailing guts
like glutted blue ribbons.
Some had shattered bone
thrashing in sockets of flesh
like swizzle sticks.
Some were spinous
with splintered slats
they'd ripped from the walls of boxcars.
Some were grinding their ruined snouts
in the earth
or rubbing their busted haunches
against the embankment,
and some lay panting paralyzed
wild-eyed, frothing at the mouth
while local kids poked at their sides

as if they were prodding ant hills.
How they laughed
when the pig tried to move.
How they resented
their scolding fathers
gathering them
moving them away.
How they longed
to climb into the dark cars
and look boldly
on the horror, the horror.

Red Barns

Last century
there was blood in the paint
on the boards of these barns.
Ontario, I have seen
the bleeding of a slaughtered sky
in the western hemorrhage
at the death of the day
in the morbid menses
of a moon-timed afternoon
and thought of beauty dying
where it rubs the world away
in that the last of light
while somewhere else along the waking curve
young hours
warm the latches
on a dreaming door
and though a distant window sulks with rain
and pond mist
drifts like something burning slow
among the singing fogs
the blackbird's flashing wing
wags off the weed in flame
and dove flutes
mourn their flight

ah, moralizing angels, pass above these mortal barns
they bear the proof of lambs
gone silent on our knives
they have the memory of hog's lament
the sorrowing away
of market sows
the knackered beast
who proves his barrow's heart
is emptied as a well-squeezed rag
and all the sweeter crimson drums
have dripped dark zeroes full to the flux
that's quivered to final stillness in the ox
as thirsty cedar waits
to the very mow-boards
of these family farms
we've ghosts enough
to last us into unborn dust
make ashy berms from all romance
the fertile strangers yet to meet
and couple and decline
and this an awful art
behold the pigment of each generation's fate
red barns have much to expiate.

Dinner on a Hot Day

During dinner on a hot day
my sister and I watch
sweat that
sits on the tip of his nose. Every
once in a while
a small bead
plit
in his mashed potatoes
then much later
struggling not to
plit
again.

It may have spoiled our appetite
but it taught us
the meaning of suspense.

One Morning In January

We watched the dog spinning
like a fly on its back
in a window sill.
The dog's hind end
was paralyzed by the big wheels
of the gasoline truck
that twisted his spine like a green stick.
He watched the dog
spinning in the snow
his front legs madly working
his body in circles
until finally
he learned how to move
in a straight line
dragging his hind legs
like a sled.
In a month he could climb
or run so fast
his back flew in the air.
Still
one morning in January
he died
the stiffness passing through him
like frost.
Tom's eyes thawed
that morning and
he didn't watch and
the dog didn't move
until someone dragged him
like a sled
into the melting sun.

The Funeral

In the field
he digs a hole
to bury Tippy.
In the same hole
he will bury
three runts
a sow
a heifer, a bag of twine.
This isn't sadness.
He loved the dog too much
to let him go so easily.
First he pushes in the old sow
rolls her with his foot
she drops
and I hear a plop.
Water in the ground, water in her belly.
Then the runts are toppled
each with a curse.
The heifer takes a tractor and a chain
since he dug the hole so far away.
He almost lets the left rear wheel
slip in.
Then the bag of twine.
He leaves Tippy on the ground
throws in two or three shovels full of dirt
stops
looks around
to see if anyone is watching
picks up the dog
kisses him on the mouth
and lays him on the grave like flowers.
Tom doesn't cry.
He still speaks of Tippy
in the present tense.

When He Plays Harmonica

When he plays harmonica
his eyes get wild.
I've seen that look
in a sheep's eyes
when its head is caught
in a fence.

When he plays harmonica
he quivers slightly
like a piece of paper
in the hands of someone
making a speech.

When he plays harmonica
it is as if
he were breathing into
the hard mouth
of a half-drowned child.

After he has finished playing
I notice
the greasy bruise
on the silver casement
and the tiny beads of spittle
clinging to the wooden keys.

The Well

Tom peed the bed. For a boy of ten this was unusual. His father warned him
not to pee the bed again or he would hang him upside down in the well, but
Tom couldn't help it. His father hung him upside down with a rope tied
around his feet. He dunked his head like a doughnut in coffee. This was the
only justice Tom's father understood.

*

Tom hung upside down like Mussolini, just for peeing the bed. He
stayed that way for twenty minutes so he'd learn his lesson well. He didn't

dream when he wet the bed, he just didn't hold on. Down he dunked again his father cursing him on the other end of the rope.

"Piss the bed again you dirty little bastard, next time I'll drown you."

His father never lived to drown him. He died in bed and his mother remarried. A much better man and Tom says if his father hadn't died he'd have killed the bugger. Says this with his gums stuck out and his lips set.

*

His father hung him upside-down in a well as if he were a pail. He dunked him so the water ran in his upside-down eyes and ears like seeping through holes in a submerged can.

"You piss the bed again you little bastard and I'll kill you."

Tom's mouth opened under water and he couldn't scream, though the water screamed. Up he came again to his father's words "teach you." His father tied him off and left him for twenty minutes dangling like a bat just above the dark still stench of the old well.

*

The well was on ground level and it was usually covered by a board held down by a grey stone emery wheel about the size of the wheel of a wagon. The rope was tied to a pine tree by the well and white chickens pecked at the grass just a few feet from where Tom dangled quiet as a pail for fear that if he shouted the rope might snap or his father might dunk him again in the dark black water.

Sweet Tooth

Tom had a sweet tooth, or sweet gums since he had no teeth. He could sit in his room and eat ten chocolate bars in an evening. When someone asked him about it he would brag that when he was young he could eat twenty or more if he could afford them.

Once when Tom was in town Ben Bennett bet him he couldn't eat twenty chocolate bars, and said that he would pay for the bars to prove it. Tom was glad to take him up on the bet. He downed the twenty bars in short order, then he went back to work stooking sheaves of grain.

What Tom didn't realize was that each of the chocolate bars was laced with laxative. When he got to the field he felt sick. While he was crossing the stubble, cramps attacked him so suddenly that he barely had time to make it to the cornfield where he dropped his pants and shit black as licorice. He barely wiped himself with corn leaves when the cramps attacked again. And again and again.

As if this weren't enough one of the many times he wiped himself he used nettles and stung his ass something awful. If you mention this to Tom now his gums set hard and he curses the bugger who paid for the bars. But then he didn't suspect a thing.

Some Stories

Some stories Tom remembers well. Once when he was young he fell in love with Sarah who worked at the five and ten. My uncle and his cronies convinced him to shave his eyebrows off to look like a real Casanova. He bought flowers and a box of chocolates and went courting. He waited at the end of Sarah's lane for her to come home from work. When she spotted Tom she began to walk real slow. Tom waited. She seemed to crawl she walked so slow.

Just before she got to the lane Tom heard a shot. He turned around, unable to raise his eyebrows in surprise or fear, since he had none. He just stood there stunned. Sarah's father brandishing the gun told him to get on his way and never show up there again. Tom looked at Sarah whose face showed superior disgust, looked at her father whose face showed confidence and superior mockery. He ran like the wind and his love ran down his pant leg in a stream the colour of the yellow ribbon on the box of chocolates.
He hid in a cornfield one mile away. After dark he returned to Sarah's, shoved the candies and the flowers in the mailbox, a victory. He spent three weeks growing his eyebrows back, and the rest of his life hating the man who told him to shave them off.

For Tom Who Had a Stroke

And he cried
though the river flowed.
And he cried
for the stupid tractors.
And he cried
for my children, their names lugubrious
as something long gone.
And he cried
behind his hand like a shy girl.
And he cried
though the lawns were filthy
with the slew of spring.
And he cried
in the polished halls
under dull uniformity of a grey light.
And he cried
for the smut dead tongue
for the clog
in his throat.
And he cried for hours shook from a sieve
of sky along the hills.
And he cried
for his toilet
dry coprolite in white porcelain.
And he cried
for his home
yes he clung to his home
like someone holding to a branch
swept along by a great river.
And he cried
for the untouchability of the earth
for the coprophilia of the gods
busy with their excrement.
And he cried
for the cultured boy
who would put him in a book
as if he were a word
as if he were just a damned word.

When Tom Died

When Tom Died
his face did
a jagged thing I'd never seen
it do before
jutting out of coffin satin
like a rude cut stone.

And I heard his voice then & there
"boysees she's cold Johnny"
and the hand crack
that used to warm him over a gas jet
I heard that too
a clear spirit voice & high sharp clap
that cards my nerve tips
to a fleece of shivers.

But he doesn't strain against the weight of death
the way he might have
were death a heifer to break to the halter.
No he doesn't raise his arms
or set his jaw
to heave the feathery darkness
from his body
that had been a perfect fulcrum
for a water pail & a hay bale.
No more the feisty physics
of a manure fork nor the dog-sweet smile.
No more the baby lover's
"She's a dandy" greeting
he gave my sister when she came home
in my mother's arms.

When he held Laura
my sister's little girl
he'd held her
thirty years too late
his smile struck down at the corners
his whole body feckless

flayed of its grain by the mean years
that came at the end.

So when Tom lay
as dead as a sheep-killed tree
and just as spare
he spoke to me
through the organ dirge
that candied his death all wrong
through the sorrowful gauze
of the minister's studied prayers
through the grey coffin lid
of a winter sky
spoke of things regained
of a rightness
we couldn't bugger up with living.

Sometimes Now

Sometimes now
on a hot summer day
a real stem-winder
I think about Tom

getting plump
in a chair
smoking his pipe
tearless
feeling about elevators
the way some feel about air travel
staying indoors
because it is a cool habit
because it is actionless
because the nurses are kind
and you never know
about people.
This much we have learned.
You never know about people.

The Bare Facts of Morning

Here are the bare facts of morning:
this blue, this yellow, this white,
this motley intervention of builded colours
squatting on the foreground
as if to sniff the path of vision
from the minded world.
Far from the garden
we are born,
but the smell of earth
might stiffen our resolve
to live within the flesh awhile.

Accept the heart's unweeded stone
       dance within its shadow
like a flame.

Accept the mind is such a muscle
       to go flexing in the dark
like wingless beetles in a high dish.

Accept this egginess of light
       that sticks to the world
       and makes its shapes involve us
like breath across an open wound.

The Boy With the Duck on His Head

The boy is five, running for the farmhouse with a duck on his head. The
duck is flapping his wings, beating the boy's ears, hauling at his scalp like a
storm shingle hiking its nails. The boy is running, the duck on his head gyrat-
ing like a tin roof half torn off, the bill drinking blood. The boy is running,
his mad hands flashing like a feather plucker in the belly down, the duck
cleated so the toe webs are stretched open and rubbery, adhering to the flesh
below the hair. The boy is running for the farmhouse where his grandfather is
at the gate jacking the manure from his boots, first one, then the other, so the
sheep dung is there on the jack blade whickered with straw, and dark green,
lincoln green, cud green, apple-shit green, a high sweet rose-garden stink

instant and to be relished. The grandfather says nothing. With his eyes says, 'Don't hurt that duck, boy.' Says, 'Ducks are money.' With his eyes. Turns. Walks towards the house. Leaves the boy with the duck on his head like a living hat.

Hod Full of Stones

"When they built this house," Herb'd say, patting the arms of the easy chair to signify that he meant the house he was in, "the brick layer worked with an exact number of bricks. It was the assistant's job to load and send up the right count so the tradesman could finish the row." Herb'd pause and draw on his pipe so it rattled his spit like a page shook out to dry the ink. "The bricklayer was high on the wall, so he was haulin up each section's worth with ropes. He was pretty much at the mercy of the half-wit who was helpin him on the ground. Well, he got to sendin up and down for bricks like he was drawin water from a well with a wooden bucket. He kept that lad humpin till he couldn't manage an even load cause he ran out of bricks, and when the bricklayer got to jerkin the rope demanding enough for the next tier, the boy yelled up, "Send me down three bricks, will you Seth, so's I can fill up me hod."

Herb'd lean back in the chair then, smiling and puffing himself into a nest of smoke like a ram with too much wool on his forelocks. Can you measure a man by the stories he chooses to tell, the way he chooses to tell them, and the point he makes in the telling? I don't know. I suppose we were meant to laugh at the boy who didn't know better. I'd be inclined to say, "Get your own goddamn bricks" and leave the bugger on the wall jerking his rope with his hod full of stones.

The Day the Devil Came to Highgate

Once a troupe of black evangelists come to the village. One fella preached till he got so hot steam was rollin out through his shirt. Well, I never did go in much for hell-fire and brimstone, so when I heard him conjurin the worst of Revelations, and them choir girls got to wild-eyed weepin and gnashin their teeth like horses in Gomorrah, I come up with a plan.

I snuck into Highgate hotel where they was stayin and secreted myself under one of them black women's beds before she got back. Now, I swear I never peeked once while she tinkled the commode. And I hardly breathed when the springs sagged down and touched my belly. It took her a half hour or more to get settled, but when she got to sawin logs real steady like she was buildin a fence, I took a good holt of that iron bed frame and shook it till it bucked like a heifer snubbed for gettin her horns cut. Well she jumped up screechin and hollerin, "It's da debil! It's da debil!"

The preachers have quit preaching hell. The Reverend Cross and Canon Smith both. But the book of thought is never closed. What people believed then, whatever they believe now—it was worth spendin a night or two in jail just to hear that woman screechin, "It's da debil, it's da debil." That was sixty years ago when the Prince of Darkness come to Highgate.

Herb Lee's Tweed Suit

Woot Hardy made me a beautiful tweed suit. He made me three pairs of pants at fifty cents a pair. An awful price for pants. Highway robbery. But they was tailored best in the country. I even had my picture took in them duds. I was gallused and gussied up like a city lawyer. I coulda robbed any simple farmer in the country and they'd of called it justice long as I was wearin them clothes and I wore them clothes back in the days when I was runnin cattle and sheep from the old country.
I was over to London stayin at a hotel in a room I shared with fella named Mr. O'Leary. A real friendly guy. He could oil his hands without touchin his hair. A good talker. We did have some pretty high times. Well when he got sight of that suit I swear you'd a thought I was the King of England.

"Oh, that's one fine suit you have there, Herb," he'd say rubbin his hands like they was frost bit. "Oh my that cloth—so richly woven," he'd say, "so finely cut," he'd say, "so stylish, yet so serviceable," his voice smooth as peeled plums. It was like he was tryin to sell me my own suit the way he went on, touchin the material like it was wove with gold. I guess I shoulda suspected something, but I didn't, cause I thought we were friends.

Anyways, I always sleep in the raw and when mornin come and I went to get my suit from the closet there weren't nothin there but O'Leary's shape. He'd left me his own cheap, shrunk down stuff and high-tailed it like a dog with kitchen scraps. I felt about like a pawn-broker's best customer puttin my long limbs in them short pants. I had four inches of white calf to spare and my arms come outa the sleeves like one of them performin circus monkeys. I coulda washed myself wrist to elbow and not dampened the twill. It musta looked as if I'd grown in the night. If I'd of flexed my shoulders I'd of split a stitch in the coat, collar to tail.

Needless to say I was ready to kill O'Leary if I ever saw him again. I ate breakfast and went about my business cause I had things to do. Well if I didn't catch sight of that same Mr. O'Leary comin on real loose and dandy in my fine tweeds, and me lookin like hard times come in the wrong size. I was kind of waitin for him to see me and then I'd call him out, right there in the street. Sure enough he caught sight of me, but instead of jumpin back in a doorway the way I expected, he kept on comin smilin like he owned the street.

He come right at me and says, "Good morning, Mr. O'Leary," tippin his hat like a tea cup to look at the dregs. I had to check myself twice to be certain I was still Herb. That son of a bitch had on my Woot Hardy tailored suit and he was tryin on my name as if he believed the clothes really do make the man, or then when they fail, words will do the trick as well.

I didn't do nothin. Just stood there my jaw slack as if the hinge had lost its bite, hand gangly in my coat as if the dirt couldn't quite keep the root. I be damned if there weren't two Mr. O'Leary's and two Herb Lee's right there in the streets of London and I just stood there tryin to get it straight in my mind which one was wearin whose suit.

Politics

Some fellas just
put their politics in the soil
and it comes up
corn.

Laurier was like that.
He worked this nation
like fertile ground
's why I got his picture hung
in every room in the house
just like them Roman Catholics

with their cruci-fictions.

(Old Syd Tape said to me once – "Never seen but one real Jew in my life, but most of them Jews is Catholic anyways—ain't they, Herb?")

Laurier would've made a good farmer.
He always checked the posts
before he strung the fence.

(I asked Bill Napp, "How's the family, Bill?" "Good Herb," he said. "Couldn't be better," he said. "I got eight kids, and all but three of em's sound.")
Sir Wilfred mighta been a funny lookin
little bugger,
and French too,
but he had grit,
and he was a real talker.
Nation builder. Not cheap neither.

(Not like Nun Little. He was so cheap his change purse squeaked like a pantry mouse every time he squeezed it. Doc told him he'd have to have an operation or he'd die. "How much'll it be, Doc?" he says. Doc told him. He went over to Digger Thompson's—priced a funeral—come back—told Doc to never mind. He'd die and save himself a few dollars. When it come time and his wife Jennie went to square things with Digger—it turned out to cost eight dollars more'n Doc woulda charged to make him sound. Nun'd ciphered wrong. I suspect he's still spinnin in his grave like a power drive on a corn picker over that.)

Laurier was a hard worker,
smart too,
knew if you cut your own wood
it'd heat you twice.

(I was over to Yorkie Pringle's and he was lazy as a cut boar. Hardly knew if it was night or day, rain or shine, summer or winter, cause he was too lazy to look outside. He was sittin in a chair one side of the room, long log shoved in the stove, burnin on the end till just before it dropped in two, then he'd shove her in a little further, like tryin to bull a two year old heifer, and shift his own business a little closer, doin that all day, every day, all winter, every winter, sparks flyin out of the stove like a camp fire.)

Laurier'd surround himself with good men,
strong men, men of character,
men who knew their jobs,
knew you could count on em.

(Cob Cull got to pinin once. Hung over I suspect. So his wife Queenie sent for old Doc. Doc had a reputation for mustard plaster so hot they was like a grass fire in your chest hair—cough formula cure tasted like sheep dip mixed too strong—and he always had that mediciney smell about him, stunk like asafetida hung in a barber shop. I heard Cob'd been feelin poorly so when I asked him how he was farin he said, "Old Doc saved my life!" "How's that?" I said, "I didn't realize you were that bad." "Yep," he says, "Old Doc saved my life. Queenie got to stewin about me, so she called him up. Said he'd be right over, but he got so busy, he clean forgot to come. Luckiest day of my life. If he'd a made it, he'd a give me one of his special cures, and I'd a died for sure." Cob and I had a good laugh over that one. He's a lot like Laurier really.)

Laurier was clear, too.
He had vision. Knew what he wanted.
Not like around here now.
War's on and things around the farm
don't sit too good
so when Ken Clark asked,
"How's things Herb?"
I said,
"Things are terrible.
John's overseas,
I'm too old to work,
Ben's no good,
Tom's crazy,
and my son George is dissatisfied."

(He wants a car. He wants to buy a tractor. He wants to get married. He's out all hours playin cards. "You'll ruin your health," I said. He won't listen. There used to be a fella in Highgate. Randy Rendalds, we called him Junior. Slow as a barn tap in winter. He drug a loggin chain wherever he went. He even took it inside the hotel when he went for coffee. Luggin it everywhere like he was on a chain gang. I saw him comin down the street one day draggin that chain, kickin up dust like a harrow in dry ground. "Junior," I said, "Why are you always draggin that chain?" He stopped and looked at me like that was the dumbest question he ever heard. He says, "Lot easier draggin it than it would be pushin it, Herb." And he don't even laugh. Just walks away, like a horse does when you run out of sugar. George got that tractor. It does the work of twenty horses. John come home safe and settled back in. Ben died. Tom's still crazy. And Lester B. Pearson's no Laurier, no matter what anybody says.)

Things My Grandfather Did

At times I hated my grandfather, Herb Lee, and could hardly wait for him to die. I am not proud of this. I was perplexed when others called him 'great.' At his funeral when someone said, "It must be very hard to lose him. You must be very sad," I might have replied, "No, not hard, not sad, but strange." I had thought he was immortal.

The first time my mother, Irene, met grampa he sized her up, grasped her hand in a firm grip, looked her square in the eye, and said, "How old are you, and how much do you weigh?"

She was 22. She weighed around 110 pounds. She didn't answer.

*

After my mother was married to my father she and her sister, Dorothy, were in the kitchen having coffee. My grandfather came out of the bathroom stark naked, dripping wet, drying himself with a towel. He was in the mood for conversation I suppose.

"Hello Dorothy," he said, innocently rubbing his nakedness as if he were polishing brass. He was 80. He weighed around 190 pounds. Dorothy goggled into her coffee cup choking a little as if she'd swallowed a fly.

*

My mother often said we never had a home of our own. Once when she was getting ready for service he asked her, "Why do you go to church?" pushing the question close, examining her, watching her eyes.
She did not reply, so he repeated the question, "Why do you go to church," catechizing her while she fastened her Sunday hat on her hair.

27

She turned and left in silence while the question came a third time, falling like an unspied sparrow behind her.

There are some things you do not ask. A lesson my grandfather never learned.

*

When his wife Stella died after forty years of marriage he said, "Is she gone then?" Spoke that simple grieflessness, as if she had merely stepped out of the room for a moment. My mother took her passing hard and memorized his words like a curse.

I was too young to remember my grandmother, though my mother said she was a good woman. And she told me often how he had used her.

What my mother meant by 'used' was that he had worked her like a draft horse till she dropped, though she died of heart failure at a goodly age. No one ever knew how he took her passing when he was alone.

*

Once he spit over my mother's shoulder into the dish water. She drained the sink. The spittle was the last thing to wash down. For a minute it swirled in the drain mouth like a dollop of hog fat.

*

He used to piss off the back porch into my mother's flower garden. The petals blanched and the leaves curled up and wilting little flowers died. He would hike his zipper, savouring this small victory over women's ways.

*

When he was young my grandfather had black curly hair. "Nigger hair," his sister Mabel contemptuously called it. "I'll bury the old bastard," she said.

All the strong women knew it was better to be born a sheep than a woman on the farm that had been in the family since the early eighteen hundreds. Mabel was no exception so she'd moved to Toronto when she was young, and near the end of her life dyed her hair blue.

Once grampa said to her, "Mabel, why do your eyes look so wild?"

"Man," she said, "you don't recognize beauty when you're looking at it."

*

My grandfather, the shepherd, the cattleman, the gentleman farmer, loved and admired by his fellows, my grandfather and Mabel fought all their lives. "I'll bury the old bastard," she said with her sky blue hair and rouged cheeks.

28

It seems the rivalry stemmed from a time that he accused her of burning the old house down as a young woman. She smoked cigarettes, drank strong liquor, read important books, and was proud and bold as any man. She was a Lee, and as my mother often said, all the Lees are strange.

Only Mabel stood up to Herb and put him in his place. She saw him real, she thought, no myth, but a reflection in a smoky mirror, she looked him in the eye and cursed his damned stubborn hide, "I'll bury you, you old bastard."

*

When Mabel died she was cremated. Her blue hair, rouged cheeks, fine mind, and strong will all burned to ash; all dead and gone. After the burial service my grandfather walked across the lawn to the gravestone, picked up the urn, shook the ashes next to his ear, and spoke: "Mabel, Mabel, are you in there Mabel?"

He spoke solemnly, struck by an awful possibility. He listened, the urn held next to his ear like a conch. There was no sound, either of the sea or a soul.

*

The first thing to change was his signature. The pen made an ever more ragged trail, the name eventually disappearing into a scribble, without strength, without sense.

*

In the last year, he had to be helped to the toilet. I can still feel his hand landing on my arm like a claw that hauled him up from his nest. Bird boned, he leaned on that arm, shuffling across the room to where he bent and settled in a clatter on the seat. Then he'd strain, his waste coming dry, like some large and jagged egg.

*

"We're going to have to put you in the hospital, Herb," Old Doc said to him when things got bad.

"No you're not," he said. "I want to die at home."

*

On the last night of his life he said to my father, "George, I'm starting to feel a little better. Could you ask Irene to make me a big breakfast." My father took the tray of hot food into his room in the morning and found him there,

cold. Later I heard my father's voice on the phone through the closed door—
"Dad's gone," He said,—and his tears.

So be it. Despite it all, I miss him.

*

When Em bathed his body after he died she said, "He didn't have a single
bed sore." I think of her turning the soapy cloth in the folds of his unblem-
ished flesh. A daughter's ablution. His cold heart. The strange stillness of his
eyes.

*

After the funeral we went into his room and pulled out the drawers full of
black and white photographs. We burned most of them. We did not know
who the people in them were.

The Men

When the men come in from thrashing there is the wet hubbub of washing in
the outdoor tub. Their golden forearms, their grit-rimmed napes, the knob of
their spines articulated like old hickory. They talk gaily of the golden blast
that knocked the tiny hired man mowing backwards in a thick wind. And the
laughter as he comes houseward after like a scarecrow come to life half-
stuffed. And he washes last leaving the water black and murk and well-
strawed.

And they come in through the kitchen for the middle room. Doffing
their caps where the table is heavy with harvest in the cool dark centre of the
house. And they do not mind the work of women. They expect busy daugh-
ters and rapid invisible wives. The platter of beef floats by in a circle rushed
light with hunger. The potatoes pass from clouds into a blink at the bottom
of the bowl. The vegetables reconfigure in smaller portions. The bread shrinks
on the loaf. The butter melts back in a yellow retreat like heated gold. And of
a sudden the seconds come. The pattern dresses fly about in happy servitude
working the crowd of bellies, working the thirsty crew. And the men lean
back. Loosen their posture notch by notch. Apple down the length of them-
selves to the laces. Lean back and pick their teeth. And lick the syrup from
their spoons.

One fellow pulls a fieldmouse peeping from his pocket. Dips him like a
candle wick in the maple syrup at the table centre. The rodent goes hip and

shoulder sinking in the super-sweet darkness. And the prankster tips back his
head, lowers the wet mouse in his own wide mouth, and pulls him out clean.
He mumbles laughter looking to the women for the shock of it.

But Stella hides her disgust. Clears the table in sour silence. Begins the
afterdance in the happy absence of men. Gathers back the ruin. Pours away
what's left of the syrup like the unwatched passing of afternoon light.

The Mind is a Glass-Touched Ocean

I want to hold time fast
and gentle
as a beetle does a crumb
and in the grand simultaneity
of the past
where birth and death
are overlaid
like the incidental blending
at dusk and dawn
when the words moon and star
and stone and human
meet as in the kissing together
of pages
in the movement of breath and lips
and I feel the past in my own oldness
at the centre
of what was and what is yet to come
though others see my face
without the boy
and I think of grandmother Stella
and say the word girl
and see her
plum-smooth and naked
bathing in her mother's kitchen
the wet sheen of a child's beauty
in the shiny soap light
where bubbles break
like someone weeping softly to herself.

And if I say the word
woman once and first
I see her
eyes fixed on her studied hand
the small teacher-driven movements
of a shifting pen
the coffee flavour of the hour
fading where daylight
throws itself like clear water
in the air.

And over a life of nouns
from bride to wife to mother
birthing in the blood-wet bed
to mother
sending her children to school
launching her elder son to war at sea
dying into memory
with the mind become
a glass-touched ocean
where the wonders can't be seen
beneath the beautiful
light-wet surface of the waves
though there's bountiful colour below
the here and now
in the now and then
if you touch your face with open eyes to the blue.

The Woman with the Hem of Her Coat Hanging

With the hem of her coat hanging
the woman is walking home from the village
after the rain the crooked river of her stockings
follows a vein to the heart.
She carries groceries
for her husband
and her heels hammer
the gravel

with a purpose of miles
like a child learning to build
on the rounded shoulders
of the road.
Hers, ditch music
blue chicory and wild carrot
corn stalks
wealthy green dancers
in a soft-whispered waltz of summer wind
the wheat field's golden worry
and the boys hoe dog bane
from beans in the heat
while she with her embrace of sugar
the small sweet child of the sack
asleep in her arms
with the dead-weight drift of a dreaming daughter
and the broken stitch in the hem
makes her seam importantly poor
a small philosophy
of garment rather than want of style
she talks in silence
to the world of mending
our way
in the rather this than that
of her choosing
not for the gossip of dogs between barns
nor the bull bellows
above the door below the mow
but she thinks with hands to the eggs still warm
like lights turned low in a room just left
and she muses on the seen darkness
the mother-safe hour
after understanding
when sureness deepens
and concern swings its precious circle
round a single house.

A Slow Magnificance

There is a slow magnificance to life.
One day you are a girl
sweeping out your father's store
with a lazy broom
like a river willow
and wondering what you'll be
the next, it seems
the night weight of a slumbering moon
aches with the pull of blood
and you are mother
once, stillborn, twice
a swollen beauty
with a promise and a wish
and all the work to do
in the doctor watch
as it is with a fever vigil
in the long
and drawn-out darkness
the stars configured
like hen grain in the heavens
and you have a nameless child
and you have a daughter
and you name her Mary
and you name her Stella
and you have a son
and name him John
for John his father's father
and the next child, Emily
and the youngest: George
and four born before and between as grief
is sister to five joys
and their little souls
wet-fire off into the air smudge by smudge.

And so, already mother
to your mother's brood
now mother to your own milk
and they grow

and then you mother
your children's children
in the years to come
after the pony hours
that a boy might spend
racing in an apple wind.
 And now
the trees are gone
the cross-cut stumps stand
like low white tables
in the orchard
as chord by chord
the winter smoke perfumes
a future heat
in a cider redolence of country autumn.
I see
a woman
with a tiny creature
stepping in her womb
the flutter of a foot
beneath the gourd-round belly flesh
become the septugenarian shepherd
pausing at the gate
to check his sheep
his boots not tied
fanned out against his legs
he walks
the wolf's opinion of the world.

A Song of the Knowing of Death

I sing a song of the knowing of death
beside an intelligent stone
and though I fail to remember, I revere
the mourners' faces
drooping there like jam-jar lilies
to grieve the weight of sorrow
and say to the grass

hold fast against the summer
keep faith beneath the snow
though there is no heart in this little hill
no health below the grain
nor in the oaken swell
where earth might tell us all
the cold that crystals in the clay
and makes a rock
of February land.
And is it lonely to be dead, I wonder
woman wombed by heaven, among moon milk
and the mammal stars
your name and both your fatal dates
frame the full and chiseled
knowledge of your life.
What did you do with yesterday
but lie about tomorrow
and take the ease of feckless bones
no more than gathered sticks to most
museums, I'd curate
like a son, I'd steal the smoke
and hold it
as one concealed afraid to breathe
for fear of being overheard
and then the cocktail singer
with his jazzy cool exhale
I'd say and say
"see here, the spirit lives forever"
though all their monuments
weather into one mirage
and the stones go smooth
and break against a jaw of grass
when every memory fails the face
even then
the temporary presence of each life
is sacred
and the universe improved.

And All the Clocks the Same

There is no coherence to a life.
No pattern
from the past.
All stories
falsify.
All futures flit about
like sparks
that mostly fail to catch.
And of remember when
and of imagine what
and of the rush to be
she was, and is
and shall have been—
a photograph, a scent,
a touch, a dream,
a day the sunlight
caught the shadow of a door
the darkness
seen beside the light
the weight of both
within the mind
the left to see the right say
one whisper
and the candle strays
and strains to hold its flame
one smoky wither like a wisp of hair
one final ember on the wick
one blink
of truth to know
cold fire by
and all the bony fuel of life
used smooth
as worry stones
the soft parade of ghosts
mere chimneys in a winter sky
black windows looking in
on all the clocks the same.

The Strapping

Teacher was at the back of the classroom tapping her shoe. I had not heard her yet. It was lunch hour and the rules were very clear, very strict, and very severely enforced. I was having fun. I was showing off. Everyone was laughing at me. I liked it best when the girls laughed.

I had taken my wax paper sandwich wrap and twisted it into fake cattle horns which I held to my forehead with one hand. I could still smell the mild scent of peanut butter in the paper. I was making loud bull bellows and rushing around the room from desk to desk gently nudging here, pawing and snorting there. The boys waved rags of torn lunch bags. I ran like a wild bull up and down the rows of desks. The girls backed up in their desks. Tucked in their scarred knees. Giggled. I thumped them. Beat at them like a nursing lamb. There was commotion. There was nonsense. There was shenanigans. There was chaos.

Teacher must have heard it from her teacher room. Perhaps she'd lain aside her own egg salad. Perhaps she'd set her coffee cup down with a thunk. Perhaps she'd screwed the thermos lid down tight, arisen and walked to stand in the doorway, tapping disapproval. For there she was tapping her foot at the back of the classroom. And the class fell silent, one by one. I did not notice much until I saw the shocked look on Shirley's face. I saw the blush of her cheek. The gape of her mouth. The trembled motion of her chin. The silence fell upon me like a web. It stuck to my face like a bubble blown too big. I felt Shirley's ribs go bump. I backed up and bumped again. I saw with my crooked eye how she sat suddenly erect, smoothed her gingham dress over the pink scars of her knees, folded her hands before her on her desk as if she meant to build a church of fingers. She was innocence. She was doll stiff. A child of rectitude too certain to ignore. I looked up and saw teacher. I felt suddenly hot. Fire flushed. Fevered. The horns molted from my guilty hand. I could no longer bear to be myself.

Teacher crossed the room with purpose. Her heels fastened nails down deep in the floor. She banged like a barn being built in the distance. I straightened up. Froze in place. Teacher reached her desk swimming the thick black-strap silence. Her desk drawer slid open. I walked towards her crooked finger. I saw the strap she held hanging down like a tail. Teacher took my palm, turned the lifeline to the light, straightened the fingers, and began the windmill sweep of heat and flame. Teacher. Adult teacher, rocked back on her heels and whistled leather. The hard thing snapped into flesh. Stung and stung again my little hand. My mouth quivered and went wet. I knew now what she meant when she'd said, "do what I say." My game had come to this. Five, I think. Five times she struck. At each blow I shuddered and winced and shut my eyes for fear. Five. Never again would I do anything wrong. Never again, I promised. Only moments before we had all been laughing. Now the room was quiet. Only the cruel children were glad of this event. Never again would I ever, ever do anything wrong. And I was six years old. And she was fifty. And never again would I ever do anything wrong. I promise. I promise. My hot hand. I promise never to play the bull again. I'll sit very still and be a good boy. I'll never laugh out loud or play the bull again. I promise. I promise. My little six year old hand hot as tea service. My little red six year old hand.

The very next day, Dick Lowell and I took the strap out of teacher's desk and pretended the squeers. Of course we were caught. And Dick's hand was like old paint before the end of the year. And I remember and refuse to forgive.

When I Was a Boy and the Farm Pond Froze

When I was a boy
once every winter the farm pond froze
wide as a field from fence to fence
we'd go down with skates, puck and stick
and play in the burning wind for days
the ice slithering with cracks
under our weight
seeping at first with water, then
collapsing in dried hollows where the furrows
cut tiny valleys
in the plough-rolled earth
till the game had shrunk to such boundaries
of ruin
we could barely turn between the evaporating kingdoms
of snow-boot goals.
Then one terrible day the whole wreckage
broken on the knuckles of frosted clods

would lie fallen like a puzzle tossed in the air.
That was the last of the generous mornings.
The last of the pond
groaning like a fat man's bed
when the wind turned suddenly cold and ordinary
and the snow scattered in filthy patches
stippled with dust.

The Swallows Used to Swoop the Cats But All the Cats are Gone

Old Whitney
with the rat-torn ear
whose heart unthrottled
was left stiff
as wet leather
where I found him
stretched out under swallow shadows
his nose tipped in dry blood.

Grey Malkin
quivered like a shy smile
held too long for a camera
the day he died.

Blackie lay
her jaw unlatched
to entrails crow-plucked
by beaks picking like women unknotting a lace
with the tine of a fork.
And all those kittens
nested blind in the straw mow
have gathered and blown away like what the mop
shook out the door.

So now I know that when life is loosed
untethered as a twilight cloud
it makes no sound
in going where it goes.

A Clowder of Cats

Bear Bell, Whitney Kelly, Mordecai,
Blackie Laforge, el muerte, Boots Buckminster,
Muller Mahoney, Eyeser Dyes, de Ted, Lemon Gin,
Sasha the Mad Slasher, Tiger Lamb,
Chopentally, Smoke, and all the nameless generations
of rag-tag barn cats
trotting with mice in their mouths
rat-notched ears
lapping the flies in with the milk
lolled on hot tin
on the threshing machine
rubbing window glass with their shoulders
padding the beams in the mow
taking the cattle yard
in the swoop of swallows.
Dying in winter
their frozen forms emerging from snow
like sculptures half-cast in plaster.
Dying in summer
where you find them
their mouths pulled tight with death
their underbellies gritty
as a flower-planter's hands.
Dying alone, a half step away
from some destination
in the crawl space
under the porch where autumn leaves gather
and webs hang down
like the torn rigging of ghost ships
beneath the bush beside the garden
on the manure pile that steams
if you lift it with a fork
or, never to be found
disappearing into the distance beyond
the distance voices travel
helpless as the jump and flutter
of birds that can't fly
and I am crying like girls behind doors

crying like the grey-white
edge of rain
coming slowly across a field.

Doorway

Framed by the doorway
in shadow
the manger hay is tangled
like the guts of a radio
Michel sees
the sheep heads
in tableau, a kind of
pool shark's mad physics
pushing light across the straw floor.
Dust shafts dropping
trajectories through perfect lenses
that catch
and raise confusion to an art.
Michel stops
transfixed.
My uncle passes by without a glance,
and Tom the hired man
claps his laughing hands
and startles God.

The Bad Philosophy of Good Cows

Like a sleigh ride it was,
throned on the old wooden manure scraper
and circling
the cattleyard behind the chug
of the orange Case tractor.

Enough to jar your bite marks
like a shook-out string of pearls
watching the green engine housing

breathing gas fumes on the wind.

Round and round we went
in a careless carousel
bucking over ice and frozen straw humps
round and round
my small body beetling the angles
like the bent hands of a pocket watch
a tiny argument
I battled dung heaps up and down
the rough-house undulations all morning till noon.

Finally done I stand atop the rank accumulation
like the only king of castle cow chip
while the cattle ungather
as cattle will when humans
are finished with their chores.

And as if to say,
"Here's enough of entropy to get you through
the toughest maize"
three heifers, and a cow
lift their tails
and have a simultaneous silage
constitutional
on the clean cement
and their big dumb muzzles moo
their bad philosophy
at the empty winter heavens.

A State of Gracelessness

Billy and I were
chasing pigeons,
clapping their wings like evening gloves
under the barn hip
until I ran
treading over the mow hole
a wingless, waxless Icarus

plunging to splash in cow flap
a dozen feet below...
an airless conflagration in the wet straw.
The poppy roan startled by this
fragment of human sky
suddenly wheezing in her dung
came to sniff me like a newborn calf
before she turned
to moo above the half door

and moo she did
a peasant mother's mournful ulularum
so loud
the cats stopped whipping their tails
over the white-washed mouse gnaws
and raced for cover.

By the time they came
to find me
I was standing
my small body shivering
and shit-brown
like a reflection in the muddy Thames.

My mother merely
made me go and shower
but the roan poppy
worried the whole night long
bellowing
under a sustained applause
of pigeons.

Shouting Who We Are

After chores
the inconsequential continent
of my father's discarded clothes
dusts the cold shed floor.

Hog-smell perfumed
with the talc of chop
puffed into the sleeves from leaning on the hopper
caught in the fine sift of their hunger
pigs nudge his boots from the trough rungs
and skid through a scarf of straw
circling like someone setting a pocket watch 23 hours wrong
then collapsing where he walks
rubbed from knee to cuff
by their hock-tinged paradigms of dung
and the bristled fabric of their hams
they race
breathe wet-snouting into the stuff he's left behind
their tongues powered like an unlicked chalk gutter.

One miffed porker crabs the door
so it kicks on its hinges
while five cylindered noses
make a pink daisy chain   00000
in the chink of light
between the door bottom and the cement stoop.

Not a lawyer
who hangs his weskit on a chair
loosens his tie, and stagily rolls up his sleeves
to address a jury.
Not a doctor
who wears his stethoscope
like a sacred necklace
touching the cold amulet to your heart.
Not a poet
bangled and rapt
buying the death of each brief moment
with the coins of his eyes
and the coin of his word.
Not a mortician
with the slow sad droop of his hands
draining from each stiff white cuff
like something frozen while it flowed.

But a farmer
up from the barn
unafraid of his nakedness
the shower raining in the little gutters of his flesh
swirls in the drain mouth
milky with what it has meant
to live this day
as we all live it
shouting who we are.

On the Way Home From the Meat Factory I Decided to Be a Poet

On the way home from the meat factory
I decided to be a poet!
Because sausages hung
like the long braids of Slavic girls.
Because the herd bull
took the worm of the bullet
in his skull
and fell like a dynasty.
Because the hogs
caught death on electric floors
and jittering were dragged still warm
in their fit's-midst
to be halved like apricots
with their blue guts spilling
a circus-clown's nightmare on the floor.
Because their heads came severed
like hill fighters
for the deli.
Because the cattle fell
like drunks in metal stocks
then were carbonnaded and hung to cure
in the time it would take
to light a cigarette in the wind.
Because blood spilled in the gutters
under the peeled beasts

and ran bubbling still hot
for the reservoir.
Because the chainsaws whined in bone
like a mosquito night
and the bandsaw cut clean portions
marbled with fat.
Because I hunger.
Because the hand that cuts the meat
feeds the city.
Because I hunger
and am human
on the way home from the meat factory
I decided to be a poet.

The Man in the Field

The man in the field
stands in the waist-deep water
of wheat
feeling it sway against his hips
like a woman sweeping her skirts
in a sweetheart dance.
The man in the field
watches the sun solve a puzzle of apple branches
in the slow shake of an easy breeze.
Sees in the drift of acres
how a butterfly comes loose
from the design
and then drops again into the huge blue pool
of things
like a stray button that follows
a slack thread
from the needle's source
to its place for the first and second stitch.

The man in the field gazes out where the dog is drowned
and leaping above the flow
looking for mice to kill

out where the bees harmonize
and swish on their fuzz
to waggle down the bead length
where the hulls knock together in a beard
like the boots of jewels.

Everything there is to know about the world
is known by the man in the field,
but when he speaks
the wind carries his words away
to whisper in the knotholes of the barn
without so much as touching the boards
and his words stay inside forever
with the hay on the bottom
like memory.

There's Nothing Like a Shade Tree in a Field of Grain

When all my verbs are tense
and sun beats hard within my head
like the heart of a time-worn man
climbing his last on a set of stairs
I know it is the hour
to put all work aside and rest
and then I think
there's nothing like a shade tree in a field of grain
to soothe these tired bones awhile
beside old Tom, the hired hand
who sits like a stubbed-out cheap cigar
in that shade
when the field is cut
and another jag is waddling
up the cow-rutted lane
for the barn.

Far from the thresher's noise
we're pitched like culled sheaves
our bodies lost

in soft grass
in heat
gone dizzy in the distance
where it shimmers like whiskey in the brain
and the kind of silence
you can not, will not
fill, comes on
when birds are still
with listening.

I Was Spreading Manure in the Summer of Love

I was spreading manure
in the summer of love
and it fell on my cap
like a movie-set rain
and I smelled of the world
and I smelled of a green-thumb garden
of the black earth
beneath the rose
and I was in tune with the field
like a dog near a hole he can't find
where mice live
and I roamed like the wind in the wheat
and leaving a swath
like a boat in the sea
where the grass crushed brown
in my wake
while the tug went light on the tongue
and the wheels rode the ruts
where the ground hogs lived
and the cattle tree
wove its leaves for the breeze
like a woman with sheets from the wash she can't hold
and I was in love
with the beauty of girls
I saw even in the whisper of clouds
as they came down to sleep in the blue

trailing gowns of vapour vacant white
and sometimes then
if I held the sun in my mind
behind closed doors
all thinking went warm and full of thin yellow light
and life was so good I could dream
it was real.

On Sunday with My Uncles

When the baseball died in the distant grass
on Sunday's of Scrub and 21 Up
I did not see
the impossible dying of my uncles
nor in the final slow wobble
of that white orb against a blade
too stiff to bend
in the last going still of dead spheres
I did not see
their avuncular enfeebled heads
rocked forward in picnic sleeps
nor the loss of joy in living
over the long wait
of being old and ill.
Nor in that fatal jump
of stitch grounding out about a stone
the startled waking in the sun
and sum and mid-sentence of a dream
of those dear men
who once were strong as the wood of bats
who kept that strength in check
for fear of wounding children
with the power of a hit nor let
the physics of their adult arms
destroy the game.
 But when they came outdoors
to share their love of play
and prove their love of us

when we were boys and girls
they tumbled through our lives
like hail through clouds
and never touched a thing
until they struck the earth.

And now a quarter hundred summers hence
and some I see them sweetly nursed by wives
who know that losing
outside the game
—is worse
than any failure to win the bases
worse than any glory
from the crack of bats
or the trebled heft of catching
what moves too fast
to catch.

Maine July 29, 1995

Red Heaven

In my mother's photographs
you see a row
of disembodied heads
above them
a huge expanse of wall, red heaven.

I remember her gazing down
with the sun on her shoulder
shading the box camera
with her hand
and then with a click
she captured what she saw
which was mostly
decapitations in Sunday best
the top of a boy's hat
my sister chin to hair
my father's seven-button intelligence.

51

And that slow camera
became a calendar of growth
and fashion
the lazy diarist of missing months
and absent winters
of Christmas juxtaposed to June
a break in the weather
a lapse in memory
a cruel jest of frost on flowers
my sister's folded white-gloved hands
floating up the house
like the timeless flight of doves
the years she grew
between lambing and calving
in the straying impatience
of light.

The Night the Simpson Barn Almost Fell

You could hear the old barn
groaning from the house
in the half light
and then the clap-chased Guernseys
came scattering out the door
because it had been a heavy harvest
and the hay tons
sheltered a dark green burden
this cattle heaven could not bear.
All day long the men had mowed the field here
squatting like miners in the tight-packed heat
as the knot holes blinked shut
board by board to the cedar hip
till they'd stooped
and raked their shirt spines
on the roof nails fanged down
and they came crawling
late into the lowing
long after the dusk had come dusting

at the windows
and they looked
to the wowing white flex
at the shuddering storm ship
of the thing
and knew the straining strength
of stone and grandfather wood
could not hold
and they worked
under the crush for hours
jacking and shoring the smothering creak
and then out
of that heavy darkness
under a farouche sky of wild and shy stars
they stood and listened
as the old barn suffered
like a broken-ribbed beast
too hurt to breathe.

Stumping

We were hauling at the stump
like incorrigible midnight vandals
rocking a tough gravestone.
I was riding the wag of it
as you would the lashing tail
of a great beast
with so little energy left
it might die in the struggle
from the exhaustion
of being held down
my father standing close by
on the green belly of the field
and Tom the hired man
joined my energy to his
so you could see and feel
where the long thews of rootwork
flexed in broken soil
the sinews snaking out
in vain articulations

like the claw-hold of a hawk in flight
carrying the earth away
towards an imaginary America
and Tom on the squat crosscut crow's nest
crying out with a thirsty hand
dropped across a century of rings
accomplished nothing
until my pyrotechnic uncle
came walking from the wagon
a casual sapper
carrying explosives
two yellow butcher's-paper wands
of dynamite
the long cowlick of runner's candles
anxious to be doing.
And then with the quick flare of a struck match
he had the loud air thick
with clods and wooden rockets
crashing on the wagon
like the skulls of luckless soldiers
and after, Tom stood in the hole to the knee
amazed and not quite
half as tall as himself
as if he'd simply sunk there
to the depth of dog sorrow
with nothing more to do
but gather back
the shuddering wreckage
fill in the hollow
where once he'd have shivered
climbing.

Urgent Things
for C.H.

How we learn
if we live long lives
about the rhythms of a lifetime—

and I add to urgent
and important things, necessity
and make of this
a wise enough completion
to satisfy, at least for now

and just a while ago
I sat on the cement verandah
near the gone
redolence of wild currant
stolen from June
by the men on the farm
who rip things out
and my mother said
aren't we three old fools
of herself and my father and uncle
we'll work til we drop
and I see
by the stagger of shadows
in a balance of pails
how half-oat heavy they are
how the peach crop comes and goes
unattended.
I remember the greenings
fallen to a brown bruise
on a cider-scented wind
touching the world by dozens
as they disappear
as then I know

my father must sell the sheep
a hundred years
since they came here first
and all things come to an end he says
and I feel
his sadness as you would
a coolness on a sunlit stone
under the slow drag
of shade
and of this necessity

of the fecklessness of true seeing
when things begin to blur
as it is with the memory of dreamers
fading into wakefulness

and as a boy
impatient over everything
not centred on myself
I was so wonderfilled
the light came off me
in a wash
where now it settles in
on my father's hearing
a dark absorbing sorrow silenced
by the bleating hills.

I Can't Believe it Myself Most Days

There Is a Nation

There is a nation in my mind
is not the land
nor salmon maps
nor memory, nor names
nor a gathering of huts
nor tracks a scar
across the flats shaking the wheat
and blasting the snow
for its share of the hills
nor ragged green pines
whistling lonely
under the dream-wet brush
of a wolf's moon-dipped tail
nor all the invented borders
no, there is
in my mind

a nation of long silence
spinning down light
as a lover's touch
telling me life begins
with all the beauty and blasphemy
of living exactly here
in the wordless landscape
of home

The Irish Famine

They died in their mountain glens.
They died in their fields.
They wandered into towns
and died in the streets.
They closed their cabin doors
lay down upon their beds
and died
in their houses.

They died in meaningless moaning heaps of ragged clothes.
The husband dies
by the side of his wife.
The child drops off forever into a filthy fit of sleep
and dies.
The father buries his little daughter
under a pile of stones
her face being the last to go
closing into the final grey clack.
They died from typhus.
They died from dysentery, cholera,
and the bloody flux
their small legs wet and faecal
their eyes wide and empty with the wild
look of large glass eyes set in dolls
before the wax has formed to shape the lid.
They died foodless
of the famine fever

some of them eating the rot
of the spoiled potato crop
eating with the doors and windows open
to heal the weeping stench
spooring from the wet putrification
but these were the lots of the starved
while export ships took to sea
full of grain
full of barley, wheat, and corn
raised on Irish land
full of cabbage, and turnip and all of it
turned from Irish furrows
to feed the coffers of the English Lords.

These were the spectres
of Skibbereen, the flesh
devoured like old leather
lifted and shook to settle over
their sharp and hungry-featured faces.

Jeremiah Hegarty
was the first to starve
dropping dead in the road on a make-work crew.
And then
Dennis McKennedy
and more, their souls
withering off their weary bones
as thin as thrice-boiled tea.

And was it the malignant bad ferries as some say
who came ashore
in the Sligo mist
moving across the fields by the sea
so the plants were seen to droop
in the damp
like the melt of slender-stemmed glass
for the doomed crop smelt in a day
in a day
so the wind from the hill
and the wind from the lazy bed

blew like the stink of the dead
where the esculent lay blasted
and useless with blight.

Or was it
the wet rot, the dry rot
the fungus, the cure
that took and stole the dig
so a man might push his thumb
through the punk
and watch the wound weep
like warm tar.

Or was it the failure of God
whose holy water
could not save the yield, even
while His priest locked the gates
of the church
refusing the masses of poor
who crept like summer flies
over dung
and died humming of heaven.

Or was it nature
winnowing her children
like chaff.
Or was it
something so seeded in the narrow skull
that it grew there
with roots too deep to pull
cracking rocks like fire
sprouts shooting up through clouds
knocking the angels away from their work
like wind-tossed birds
and piercing the sun like an over-ripe peach thrust on a stick
and holding the stars in place
like gooseberries
on a dead branch.
Was it something like pulling down vines

and finding a house lost in the green.
Or was it something like cutting through thickets
and finding an overgrown gate
with its white-feathered Gideon's grace caught
like a gull in a net
cast full of the flip of silver fish
flashing their flimsy coin
where the moon tugs at the edge of a midnight sea.

The Ear in the Mail

The ear in the mail
of Harriet Beecher Stowe
was black as a scorched tart
and in that
it had come from the head of a negro slave
and in that
it had been stunned into silence
and in that
the man who owned the ear
also owned the man
who'd lent his senses unwilling to the world
notched like a Suffolk ram
and in that
each of us might divine
the entire form and fragrance of suffering
from the breathy argument
of a single human part
as from a quiet tongue
one might conjure up the voice
and language
of the human heart
and as one might detect
the will of the hand and the way
of the knife
in the cut
that took that unhappiest of aptitudes
detached and tumbling from the post

as a pressed corsage
might tumble from a lover's book
even then by a least energetic listening
one could hear the scream of the slave
in service.

This Morning We Killed a Man, and this is How it Happened

Today, this very morning, we killed Bob Dick and stole his horses. Damn good horses too. They was almost worth it. We come up the lake shore walkin' on the sand. It was about a mile from pa's old place and the sand was froze a little, which was quite strange for this early in the fall. Bob was still in bed so we was just going to take his horses and skedaddle. Trouble was Bob's hired man Jake Tooney was waitin' there with a loaded gun like he was expectin' us. I ain't absolutely too sure, but somebody must have tipped him to the fact that we was comin'. He didn't say nothin'. Just shot Tommy Martin in the ear. How a man can manage to make any kind of sound when his brains is hove in I don't know, but Tommy fell crowin' and whistlin' like a bird in a snake fight.

None of us knew he was dead till Jimmy Hyde screamed, "J-j-j-jesus H. C-c-c-christ. T-t-t-tommy's d-d-d-dead." And then we all seen the blood come leakin' out from under his head like rum from a busted rum jug.

Jake Tooney run in the house and we made quick for cover except John Dickson who never seemed afraid of nothin'. He just walked over to the barn, unlatched the door and in five minutes come out with them two fine geldings of Bob Dick's bridled and ready to go.

We was all layin' low as dogs in the shade when Bob come racketing out onto the porch. "You lead them horses back where you got them, Mister."
John Dickson just smiled. He has a way of smilin' that says the same as when other men spit. I could see pa out of the corner of my eye. He was lyin' very still, taking a bead on Robert Dick. It reminded me of how still pa could be when he wanted to be. I'm pretty certain pa was waitin' for some sign that Robert Dick was worth killin' when somebody else shot him right on the word Mr.. Anyways, whoever it was made a mess of his face. He crashed back into the door and gargled blood for a whole minute before he expired. John

Dickson never stopped smilin'. He just turned around and walked away like he'd trick-traded for them horses. Pa eased the hammer of his piece and stutterin' Jimmy Hyde he whimpered like he was a dog locked in a gutting shed.

We buried both corpses in the same grave. It looked a little like they was huddled together to keep out the cold. Funny thing about that business. They never tried any of us for the murder of Robert Dick. And both of them horses died from pneumonia. And I heard how Jake Tooney fell in the creek and drowned. When they found him he had a fish hook in both his eyes. My guess is, he must have been usin' the wrong kind of bait.

The Legend of Peaches

It was Christmas week
and the boys marched along
at the stream Brankhorst Spruit
36 miles short of Pretoria
with the lads in a jaunty mood
eating peaches
and listening to the strains
of the regimental band playing
"Kiss me mother
 kiss your darling daughter"
and singing the smell of fruit

when the rebel Boers
opened fire
and before the British could break their lines
there were so many killed
in the withering
that a century could not name the dead
at one a year
and the bandsmen lay at their bugles
breathing blood
as their last breath struck heaven
in a single groan
like the dying drone
of the pipes
their rifles still cold in the wagon

stiff as the tossed-down stalks of harvest.

And so the soldiers were buried where they died
and legend has it
that the peaches in their pockets
burst open and
grew into a grisly line
of trees.

And this is the fruit of the grave
taking root
at the hip of the dead
or in the skull of the man
with the stone in his mouth
and the touch of his face in the earth
like the flesh of a peach
and the taste of his soul
still sweet.

If I Were A Nation Innocent of War

If I were a nation
innocent of war
my flag, the white of angels
my tongue
too soft for certain verbs
would bless the danger out of stones
my hands
would shape their shares
too pure for battle's praise
ah singer, sing a song
of vacant borders, a ghost of maps
too old to draw like lines in water
my heroes would be armed with bread
my soldiers in the wheat
like sunlit gold
and women would know
their sons were safe

and fathers would not weep for glory
nor clutch a fatal photograph
nor visit where their children fell
nor worship the white multitude
of markers on important grass
nor name their deaths
nor build their bronze demise
nor send the pricking poppies
from the coat
nor drop their paper blossoms
in the snow
like wound daubs come unstuck
where blood's too wet to hold.

And all the anger
in the language, all the anger
in a faith gone mad
and all the anger
in a recollected wrong
and all the anger of stolen land
and all the anger
in a vein of coal
and the crushed amoebas of another age
and all the anger
in the sand and waters
all the anger in the salt
below the rain
and all the anger in boats
at storm, and all the anger
in the rage of fire
and a phosphorescent wind
all the anger in a mustard breath
and yellow air
and all the valiant
and all the cruel
and all the frightened
would spend their humour in a field of hay
do their duty
in a garden
and never wonder why

the loving dreamer always smiles
within the tedium of home.

It Has Quieted a Little

Poet John McCrae's young friend's last words were
"it has quieted a little
 and I shall try to get a good sleep"
and then he was
anatomized as his flesh exploded like a kicked weed
and so the story goes
it was given to Dr. McCrae to gather back the bits of boy
and like a god to shape them into some semblance to bury.
And so McCrae was changed forever
in the endless noise. Thereafter it was said
he was morose, more silent
and he went for long and solitary sorrowful rides
into the towns about Belgium
and his sad face aged ten years, and he said
"I'm dying" to himself
as if he could feel his slow heart
slowing like the deeper movements of stones in lakes
and what the larks must think of us
and why they sing to be themselves
while we weep away our human woes.

Dwindling Brothers, Dying Sons

poem on the commemoration of the Normandy Invasion

These were the dwindling brothers
and dying sons of war.
These were the disappearing strangers
who rocked at death all day
on bloated billows
like the manatee who could not swim to shore
their harp-shaped corpses
running the blood-red sea

in a double sky.
These were the death-drunk soldiers
who sank in wave beds
like buoys pulled under
by the half-drowned panic of dying young.
These were those
who went in under the roar
and strafe from the hungry beach bunker guns
slamming the strand
with man-cutting metal
sawing the spine
below the rack of the chest
so two leg stumps might stand their last
dock posts too mossy to tether a boat
what with the fellow
who owned them puzzling his foreshortened self
for upper parts
like an unplugged doll.
These were those kneeling at the pew
of the cliff
dragging the smear of themselves
against the will of a shocked heart
and broken brain
clutching the climber's rope-loop of their guts
and hoping the sand
where the kill took their souls
was worthy
as if each inch the tide crawled
like the shadow-creep
of tree shade
under a moving moon
were theirs in the loss of light
and the new cool
of shrinking into the permanent blindness
of absence.

Now is not then
and there is peace
away from the time
when slaughter stank on the wind

and cordite
stang the eyes
like the smart of swimmer's salt.
And yet we should weep
and we shall
in the broken shells of evening
we will weep
for the loss
of those who could not stay
but stayed
saying "stop there
in your lost locomotion
set rolling in the will of water."
And yet there is a grief in your name
no amount of mourning
can console
for those unsonned mothers, those disboyed fathers
reading your fate
for those unbrothered, unfriended
unlovered, uncousined
at home
and for those on the beach
in the wet weather or war
who saw you go
into the brief startlement
of being gone
still weep to think
of how your young faces tossed
in the sea
or under the grass and crosses
of Normany
where they kneel to remember
the horrible moment you went
and all the good weeks before going.

The Clearing

To work   on the farm
              in July
they came   from the POW camp
              from the war
              from the Fatherland
              from their mother's womb.
They worked in the harvest
              under the sun
              under the gun.
They sat   at the dinner table.
They were eighteen.
They were thirty.
They had eyes as blue
as China plates.
They had blond hair
cropped short as wheat stubble.

Stella had a son
in the navy
hung his picture in the dining room
over the table.
In the picture he wore his uniform
he wore a smile hugging his sister Mary.
One young prisoner
pointed with his fork
at John's photograph
smiled and said something kind
in German.
One young prisoner wept openly
under the photograph.

At dusk a truck came
to take the boys away.
At dusk the guards
poked the prisoners
into ranks; loaded them like livestock.
At dusk
the war resumed

68

just outside of Chatham
just outside the dining room
where Stella
cleared the supper dishes
under a photograph of her son
smiling in his uniform
under a photograph of her son
sent overseas   to kill such
blond and blue-eyed boys.

The Ghost of Erwin Rommel

i

A reporter compares this war
to watching fireworks over the east river
as in the green glow
of CNN we see
a solitary car crawl away along the road.
And I remember
fireflies in the two-shade dark near Bardstown
flickering a fatal summer constellation
against the ragged black
saw-toothed forest of the night
but then in this glowing box
the fertile cresent went fire red
and the earth shook
and windows shattered
and a hot concussive rush of air
bloodied the wind
as someone suddenly blasted backwards
saw flame goring the sky above the ruined street
rising to rubble
between beautiful royal palms
waving their fronds
like slave children fanning the master in the heat
as we sat at supper
watching wise men wag their jaws
to confirm the consequence of important noise.

Meanwhile, one reporter on a roof
unable to seat his helmet on his hair
dreams of a brave career
through shudders of scattering light.

ii
in Canada, Iraqi students say
"at home, the palace guard
invade our classrooms
once a week
and make a random seizure
of young scholars
whom they take away
for torture sessions and beatings
unprovoked by any other reason
but to say
'this is Sadam! the Babylonian King
reborn, and this
the furnace of his reign!'"

And so, a human madness
makes the press to show
this place so far away in space
though close in time
a sand-drift town might disappear
before our very eyes
while none of us is touched
we still see places
cheered by heartless satellites
to modify our maps
the enemy talks funny and weeps large
to make a swarthy sorrow
and we go to work
and chat
of justice and an easy victory
though families are dead
and legless orphans wait
in doorways while they die.

Green Mud

War is always the failure of the human imagination
                                                    −JBL

And in this place, this Kosovo
where hatred is at play, has been for centuries
as I remember
my Balkan history lessons
and refused then to believe as a boy
because I could not comprehend
how a lone assassin
could let loose the dogs of war
on Europe
how madness in the royals
infecting the great houses
of two Caesars
and a cousin King
could lead the sons of all
to die by tens of thousands
in the green mud and yellow gas
at crawl
between the sand-bagged trenches
where no man could live.

And now
America and all her myrmidons
at flight like gulls above a harrow
drop fire
where it does its awful work
and I fear my blood
and what it means
to be a father
when the world
would be a thief
and all the sorrows in the sweep of rain
that blur a dozen borders
below a disappointed sky
to make us wonder
who is wise enough
to stop this weather

and these mountain snows
cast shadows where the hills are cold
while children shiver in the dark
and I read and read again
where language touches language
in a kiss of breath
uncomprehended
with no poets there.

this poem was composed Monday, April 5th, 1999 while Canada participates in the bombing of Serbian Yugoslavia and refugees flood across the border from Kosovo into Albania and Macedonia

No More Need for This Old Man

There is a photograph
of a Christmas long ago
when I stood grinning
beside the guest bed
in our farmhouse
in pajamas
my hair, a slash
and I wore a pair of blue
lensless pince nez, playing doctor
touching the plastic bell
of a toy stethoscope
to my cousin's soundless heart.

Since then
my uncle died.
Since then my father's sister
breathes no more
as sorrow by sorrow
we might name them sadly
under stone.

And yesterday I heard a story
how outside a distant village

a soldier
told a refugee
who walked a weeping road
in a river of human woe
with his ailing father in his arms

"you have no more need
of this old man"

and he
learned grief
how deep it goes

"you have no more need
 of this old man"
how light he was, how small of form
how like a wormy branch
his father fell
upon himself
"you have no more need
of this old man"
and I think
I need everyone, I want them all back
those dying uncles
those perishing aunts
those cancerous cousins
that baby sister
those generations of ash and dust
my best friend breathing
in his father's mouth
listening for his heart
like placing his ear to a horseless hill
with the wind in the grass
when the cruel rains come.
                 April 30th, 1999

Living in the Red Dust

Some say it was
the sand-bagged bauxite
that made the soldiers ill
and not the blood in the soil
nor the ash on the wind in the mind
while weak water crossings wowed
with walking
like the ribs of sobbing fathers lying down
with their sorrows gone deep
from dying children.
And what smoke floats
above a fatal village?
What burning horses do we see
when we view them
shaped by flames about the withers
and their red manes leaping
where the fire seems the soul of shoulders
stallioning down to one deep Persephone
of loss.
And all the sewer lines
erupting along the bomb-bulged boulevards
of eastern Europe
heaving their sess in a poisoned street.
And all those metal birds
above them
invisible inhabitants of anonymous night
those black angels
of America
with Wisconsin pilots
whistling a long release
above the sudden lapse of bridges
the citizens collapsing and fluttering away
like wet cigarette papers
licked by rains
about their weeping mouths.

And they ate and slept
for months

those soldiers living in the red dust
of the Balkans
and the Black sea
where cold kelp clung to the rocks
like darkness
to the newly dead.

Sibling Rivalry

How can I explain to you
my nephews
that I wanted to
beat your mother's brain in with a broom.
How do I describe
the urge I had
to beat her senseless
with a door
I tore splintering from its hinges.
Shall I say
how I wished to drown her
face down
in the bathroom sink
her hair floating
her fingernails blue.
Dare I tell you
how often
I strangled her in the car
squeezing her windpipe shut
like a plastic drinking straw.
If I told you I dreamed
about the bumpy ride
up the stairs
her head thwacking against the steps
how it left lesions on the brain
you could read like Braille
would you still trust your uncle John?
Would you ask your father
to kill me
just to be on the safe side?

No Contact Hockey

We cure
the firehall blues
with booze

after we've hung our skates to dry

we talk about accidents
checks
slashed faces   eyes carved out.
One year
Al saw a boy die on the ice
his jugular cut
and pumping red.

But mostly we talk about scoring.
The easy grace
in the best of us
swiveling into perfection
only then
when the puck arcs past a shoulder
or slides cool and swift
along the ice
to tangle in the netting
like a hard black fish
that darts of its own accord.

We get drunk
on victory
smashed
on defeat
and when we go home to our wives
tired and drained with the telling
of the same stories
in as many ways as we can conjure
we go with the knowledge
that we will pay dearly tomorrow
for the glory
we hooked tonight.

Is There Anyone Here Can Blaze a Trail

Why not climb to the left of the ladder?
Enough good reasons
I suppose.
Why not sail beneath the water
holding your breath
and steering across the flow
your sail cloth heavy
your topsail cutting the surface like a shark fin?
Why not walk under the bridge
across the river
appease the troll
smile, perhaps even shake his furred hand?
Why not tip your hat to Curly Howard
and walk into a wall?
Why not strap engines to the elevator
and blast off past the top floor
or drill it below the basement
into the magma lounge?
Why not walk into the furnace
and see who gets burned?
Why not get lost
like a radar blip travelling off the screen
imagining a room full of panicky generals?
Why not burn all your maps
tramp your compass
fill up with blue light
erasing your jet streams as you go
cut loose your coordinates
so they drift down like balloon strings
and float away over the city

Events Have a Way

See Mike in the channel
his boat dragged by a dogfish
surfacing and barking like a bloodhound
after bear.

This was the sixties
when I was in a washroom in Detroit city
a frosty carp in a halo of angel fish
toking splifs
their dreadlocks welking
their eyes red with swallowed hooks
their fists dangerous from body music
standing by the urinals
yellow taffy streaks on alabaster
the grates a pool of spawning cigarettes
that die with an ugly hiss
like struck snakes.

This was the sixties
when the Beatles landed laughing in New York
and Murray the K
was fast talking like a train
running over a flattened penny
and the streets of America
were boiling with national guard
and single-minded assassins.

This was the sixties
when Philip left the county fair
to run from the kitchen palaver
of short-order cooks in a Dresden greasy spoon
for Vietnam to blotch his boots in the Mekong
and come to understand that staying alive
is a cruel jest
his brain a stain of alcohol and death.
This was the sixties
when farm boys fell in love with speed freaks
and every river rat with hands
would form a band
and even rich girls with reputations to keep
might drop their pants
and the g's from their participles.

This was the sixties
long before the angry gap-toothed insurrectionists

would cut their hair
and join the chamber of commerce
long before the gagged black boxers
would get too mumbly
for public conversations
long before a certain working-class hero
would die in a mocky drag
while a dough-faced fat boy
sat on a curb catching children
long before we'd crimp and manicure
our perfect money-green lawns
all of us biting our coins
like cynical merchants
all of us
checking our children's diets
and drinking aspartame in our tea.
This was the sixties
with Mike in the channel
riding his boat like Queequeg
behind a mean dogfish
and me in the washroom
in Detroit unraveling my face, my life in the mirror
like a loose multi-coloured thread.

I Was a Green Boy with Those White Room Blackbird Red Neck Purple Haze Blues

And I had an Afro
that would fill a door
and I wore
always open and floating because the buttons wouldn't hold
an indigo-blue Canadian air force great-coat
with huge mother-knitted mittens
the colour of thistles
at the height of summer
and I wore a long purple scarf
trailing at the throat
like Goethe skating in Germany

and I wore
pink bell-bottom trousers
and flowered shirts
and I was the Brummel of weird
I was the tangled garden of winter
I was the quintessential manifestation of music
I was the Sturm und Drang
of an orchard in storm
enough to rattle the ladders
and dump the pails
and I was as full of poems
as Dylan Thomas's grave
and we sat in the cafeterias of the seventies
and spoke like muses
over coffee and beer
and we were all promise and wish
with flesh like silk
and wild minds that took to the wind
like the white whip of snow
and John Kennedy died and Malcolm X died
and Martin Luther King died
and Bobby Kennedy died
and Al Wilson died
and Jimi Hendrix died
and Janis Joplin died
and Jim Morrison died
and John Lennon died
and Ronald Regan didn't
but we never gave in to grief
with nothing to regret
when poets had voices
and people had ears.

Why Some People Retire
for Roger

When Gill Golightly
cut his fingers in with the chops
he sawed them through
like a carpenter
jigging nails in with the wood
so they sat
in the butcher's paper
like cigar stubs thrown away lit
and he held them high
for Mrs. Quinn
poked in the meat.
The stroke had cut the circuit
in his bad arm
so the first surprise
when he held high the mess and said,
"Take a look at these babies."
was Mrs. Quinn
keeling backwards in a senseless thud
like a broom handle.
Still, the nonplused Golightly
leaning over the counter
didn't know what the fuss was about
till Jonesy coming in said,
"Gill, you've gone and sawed off
yer fingers!"

And so Gill,
looking at his hand
the end of it angled
like panpipes
decided finally to retire.

The Trade that Shook the Hockey World

When Gretzky went to LA
my whole nation trembled
like hot water in a tea cup when a train goes by.

Something about Hollywood and hockey.
Something about Canadians in Babylon.
Something about gold and the gilded blades of grace.
Something about kings in the great republic.
Something about titans and the golden gods.
Something about the myth of boys and the truth of men.
Something about beer in the holy grail.
Something about the commodity of the human heart.
Something about the fast life...
fast food, fast cars, fast women, and a fastness.
But mostly something about moving too fast in time.

The Hockey Player Sonnets

for Al Purdy

1

What about them Leafs, eh!
(e.d.*) couldn't score an (e.d.) goal
if they propped the (e.d.'s) up
in front of the (e.d.) net
and put the (e.d.) puck on their (e.d.) stick
and the (e.d.) goalie fell asleep
and somebody (e.d.) yelled "SHOOT THE (e.d.) thing
            (E-E-E-E-E. D-eeeeeeee!!!!!!!)

2

(e.d.) this (e.d.) shower's (e.d.) cold.
who the (e.d.) flushed the (e.d.) toilet?
give me the (e.d.) soap.
hand me that (e.d.) towel.
has anybody got some (e.d.) shampoo?
toss the (e.d.) over here!
thanks. what's this (e.d.) pansy (e.d.)?

who brought the (e.d.) beer?
toss me one. stop throwing that (e.d.) snow.
you could lose an (e.d.) eye.
and so on...

3

What do you mean you don't watch sports on TV.
Why the (e.d.) not?
Haven't you got an (e.d.) TV?
What the (e.d.) do you watch?
What the (e.d.) do you do?
Read!!!—who the (e.d.) wants to (e.d.) read!
too much like (e.d.) thinkin'.

there is much (e.d.) laughter at this.
and so it goes—
"what about them Leafs, eh..."

*expletive deleted

My Mother Plays Pool

my mother plays pool
like a raccoon washing a stick
the cue see-sawn
from ceiling to floor
finding a fulcrum in the snuff of flesh
webbed between thumb and finger
she plays the tapered wood
like a tough cut, a single sweet note droning
in a difficult concerto
and then lets the quiver sing
so it sometimes shoots
a blunt arrow
blurring blue chalk teats on the far wall
with a weird
billiard of small desire
a hit, a hit, a palpable hit

see those berry bruises
meant for the white ball
see how the arrow leaps
from her hand, spearing
with the sudden rigor
of an angry snake
the snub-nosed viper
no matter how I lean
and calmly show her
thus and thus
still she finds
a perilous javelin style
that Miron might have frozen, chiseled
from a second stone when his Discus thrower was done
how from her eye she squinees
and aims
how from the brave
triangulation of her arms
she finds the felt too flat
she'll be among the Amazons
or with the Zulus
banging their shields
to thump the lions out
and then
where goes the cue?
see how it waggles its length
to seek a target
mere eights might jump like numbered eggs
wishing to be satellites
in such three dimensional games
as she invents
investing all her energy
beyond the table
landing in the largest empty pocket
big enough to include
both ball and cue, and us as well
the ultimate game
she walks the green
dancing in the holograms of smoke
when the lights come laughing on.

Standing Behind Drooling Johnny
at Our Elementary School Drinking Fountain

The water is lifting and drooping
on the drinking-fountain spigot
like a glass blower's mistake
dashing in the gum-pinkened sieve
of the drain
while post-recess, the first thirsty lad
slurps and gulps
nuzzling the silver filaments
that rattle down the white dish
and swish away slow
so the teeth-dented chewing gum
floats a swirling moment
like a pastel hoik.

Behind Monkey
with grass-stain eyes,
and Chimp lick-lipping
like a dog with peanut butter on his tongue,
a couple of baseball boys
their gloves on, their heads
caught like weird upside-down fly balls,
drooling Johnny
his philtrum silky with snooze,
steps up, leans over,
his forelock slashing the rim
of the porcelain bowl,
inhales
the thick thread that mercuries the air
swallows it whole
his incisors clicking
the metal as if he meant
to gnash the chromey thing down
making foxy little nips
where it spewed
rolling his lips over the cool
dazzle
that cheek-poked him
like a dentist's finger.

Then as if bursting up
from breathless depths
he lifts his face and seizes
a sputtering patch of atmosphere
making chokey little resuscitation sounds
as if he meant
to cough a fish.
Then it's back again to muzzle
a further gallon
sucking the stream
so the very well-shine might have bobbed down
an inch or two of brick
so that when I finally stand
above
where the gluey translucence of his slobber drapes the spout
preparing to fortify myself
for an afternoon of arithmetic
I make a note of how the day
was handsome till then
racing where the sun shone clean
and the breeze blew fresh
resolve to bully poor Johnny
tomorrow
like everyone else
to make him stand last in line
the way God did
when He forged him in the womb.

Louis St. Laurent and the Sense of Things

In the early days of television
when Prime Minister
Louis St. Laurent promised the people
he would appear in their parlours
like someone peeking through a magic window
Montrealers hurried home from work
to change their clothes
for fear of being seen by him

in everyday.
And men
fastened themselves button by button in Sunday shirts
so the stiff white cuffs
encircled their wrists like lime-and-water casts
set to knit the bones
so they were pure and straight as rods
and curds of costume pearls
floated on the breathing blue bosoms
of waiting women
and children on their best behaviour
sat lick-spittled
their cow-licks weighted down
against the bob of nature
tense as springs
and bruise-kneed girls
set pretty prim and still as dolls of glass
and older sons with all the run and fuss of lads
cast into spells of brief respect were stuck upon couches
like bridegrooms frozen to the frosting of a cake
and these people
their hearts beating quick as caught sheep
as this "bon pere de famille"
appeared
lighting the way they saw themselves going
in that time at that very place
when Louis St. Laurent paid his visit
and they may well have asked
"Do you see me Mr. Prime Minister?
I am the one
in the green chair.
Welcome to my home."

Walter Mitty's Rock Video

I saw the line of her nylon tops
that circled her thighs
the way milk rings a glass

and for an instant
I was a sexy trench-coat detective
unwrapping the cellophane
from a new deck of cigarettes
for a client with honey-coloured hair
and nipples like dark cherry jujubes
in a low-cut dress
or I was a gunhand
spinning his spurs in a wild saloon
the leather gloves
plumed in my denim hip
like a brown bouquet
that trigger-fingered the air
while I swaggered
to where I owned the bar
and all the belles unfastened themselves
from sugarfoots, hayseeds,
and grocery boys and drifted my way
with their lips on fire,
or I was a spy
candling documents in dangerous weather
while back at the hotel she waited in silk
her heart racing like a mouse
in a TV room,
or I was a poet
feathering my oars in a pool
while gently Bryoning the sensibilities
of a literary femme
who kissed with her mouth open
many-petalled and sweet scarlet
like a birthday-cake rose,
pleasure-schooled in her water-lily eyes
while tiny mercury-coloured fish
call me Casanova Mitty
call me don Walter
call me famous as a river among boats
where a woman might loll in her slips
like a harbour yacht
lapping her tag lines and dreaming
beyond the buoys.

88

Jimi Hendrix in the Company of Cows

Mooooooo

ooooo0000ooooo0000oo

oOoOo

o

o

OOOOOOOOOOOOOOOOO

o

oOo

OoOoOoOoOo

mmmmmmmmmmmmmmmmmmmmmmMMMMMMMMMMMMMMMM
Mmo
oooooooooooo

ooooooooooooooooooooooooooooooooooooooOOOOOOOOOOo

OOOOOOOOOOOOOOOOO

mmm ooo mmm ooo mmm oo

mmmmmmmmmmmmm-
moooooooooooooooooooooo

n

In the News

1

Sleep softly love
for there are sheep in the news:
black sheep
menacing the fence rows,
lambs throwing bricks
on parliament hill,
a flock of rams
storming the parsonage,
knit-browed ewes
marching fleece to fleece
on Woolworth's,
drunken eanlings
sniping from the poolhall,
shearlings high on hay
tap their trotters
on the eye-glass lenses
of pretty girls in braces and training bras.

2

They are bucking in swank restaurants.
They are leaping through lenses.
They are giving interviews.
They are suspending animation.
They are simulating moon shots.
They are putting on an audience
of citizens.
They are putting on a mask
of citizens.
They are infiltrating our movements.
They are blaming our children.
They are growing casual.
They are signing off.
They are cutting their losses.
They are waiting.
Mostly, they are waiting
to stab your retina with bright lights
and plenty of action.

And though the world
would tear you through the fabric
of your sleep

dream yourself empty
darling.
Starve the world of your attention for a night.

The Curmudgeon's Apprentice

I am on the verge
of an expert disgruntlement.
I have perfected the deep twelve-toned harrumphs
of the river hippo.
I whisper epithets and imprecations
beneath the breath of love.
As it is with disappointed priests
and disapproving vicars, I moralize
my voice, low and lugubrious
as a parlour gramophone
dying in a groove.
I have managed the bitterness
of old tea
the dark tarnish of unattended silver
and the waxy orange match ends
of farmers
ruttling their ears in the evening.
I am living
at the existential rag's end
of all arguments.
I share a pessimism with the newly dead.
I practice hurling stones
at the dogs of the heart
to see them fly like barking birds
to hear them on the wind
howling above my words.

Seeking Level

I once hired a fellow
who could look at the earth
and see its bias
in the bubble at the centre of his mind
his eye a spirit level
his shoulder finding plumb
while I gophered round the crooked timbers
like a lost grave digger
setting the groaning corner beams back on stone
as we see-sawed
the cantilevered cottage going still
and now the windows true
the floors and walls meeting flush
at each soft and perfect fold
like bent paper
and I cannot believe
it was all achieved
by guess without the benefit of proof
and yet my instruments confirm
among the myriad angles of the lawn
the rise and dip of grassy ditches
the black beach tree knobbing
past the eaves
its branches ricket-boned
and I wonder how he saw
what water seeks
even in darkness
as I sit
studying the crooked blue painting
hung in the distance across the lake
where the sun goes dribbling down the western sky
like an angry man's egg.

My Cousin Sings of Wood

Of Shagbark hickory, of pignut
mockernut, bitternut and all
the other hard choices
that bring us beauty leaving
and the kind of cherry desk
that makes you sigh
and forget the jealous
conspiracy of poets
with their selfish little whisperings
of lead and ink
and know this: the large soul
is yearning at the drawer locks
of a private life
the one that keeps the sternum true
the one that shuts the sex away
in secret longing
the one like a phylactery
sliding open from the skull
above the eyes
a dreamy Dali drawer
to keep the night mouse in
some aromatic magic resin
rubbed against the bone
like the sea salt of desire
melted in the flesh.
And he plants a tree
for every tree he takes.
And so his table is the father
of an oak.
And so a golden cabinet
is mother to a river shade
where lovers sleep
a hundred years away
lost in the doweling of a distant afternoon.
And he and I
each toiling in his disappearing craft
lament a box and paper age
where I'd emblazon Dante's warning words

above the depot doors
then walk the other way
out into the genius of trees.

The Summer I Put on Siding

I'm a carpenter born
for the crucifixion of hands.
Given a choice
between steel and flesh
my eyes seem to cross
and I whack the living finger every time
as if to drive each one home
in the wood to a singular wormy flatness
under the hammer head
claw-jumping where it shudders
on the waxed-over nerve endings.

Give me a board and the best-made tools
and I'll pump
the tips like church-door manifestos.
Knock them like Christmas nuts.
Bang them till they flint black
as the best Napalese hashish.

All summer long
I've struck my fingers
one by one
as if the tune of nails
were written
for blue-note cuticles
eclipsed by bruises
purpled past the second knuckle
so the wounded nails
slipped like plectrums
milled in ice.
Oh, I've cobbled my hands
like well-made shoes.

I've tempered them like forge-hotted steel.
I've made such a contagious
co-mingling of pain
they've throbbed in shocked bunches
and leapt in the air
strobing like buck-shot birds.
Every cedar board on the house
a ten-fold violation
of helpless digits.

Where others see a building well-made
I see a pair of hands
steepled like a burning church
on the prayer-maker's pillow slip.
Where others see
the pride of a self-made thing
I see a hammer
wheeling like a gymnast
down the ladder rungs
the air hot with curses
and much thumb fluttering
the sound of one hand clapping
the look of the sunset
on the head of a pin.

They Wait in Hiding

They wait in hiding.
They keep a long and vigilant surveillance
on my suburban house.
They smoke all night in cars
and stay awake
sipping cold coffee
what detectives call mud
what cools call java, the kind
that leaves a ring in the hour
a sour circumference
of cloudy brown stain to mark

the cup's memory of evening.

And if they are women
they might leave
a dozen stale listless lipstick kisses
to flirt on filters
their bent fires gone cold
on the smell of burn.

And if they are nervous or bored
the nibbled rim of Styrofoam
signifies a gerbil's game played
against time
and in the false confetti
celebrating vacuous work
they sit like available taxis
parked against a visible curb
just beyond a most contiguous intersection
their engine grills sniffing the wind
for movement, so
that if I or anyone
should wish to back into the street
from my driveway
they might interrupt the fluid movement
of that event
by arriving with the awful synergy
of doorbells and telephones
and other seemingly random
interventions in the modern flow of worsened loneliness.

The Police

When he came rapping
I was napping.

Kid napping.

I could see him

from my upstairs bedroom window
standing at the front door
his riot helmet
straying on a randy knot of wool.
He was short and dumpy,
freshly scrubbed and deticked
his blown-dry fleece
puffing from his uniform
he looked like a plump cloud
stuffed in blues.

But I know those sheep police
are pretty hard nosed

so I stumbled down stairs
and opened the door.

"You're under arrest!"
he said,
his brain rustling behind a bony forehead.

"What's da charge?"

"Satire," he said,
snapping his hay-stained molars
importantly
on the trumped-up charge.
"It's even worse than irony
in this here state."

I was in no state to argue.
I pled guilty.

I spent six years
in the pen.

The sheep pen.
Now that I'm out
I'm sure I'm under surveillance.
Undercover sheep

bleat into their pasterns
every time I cough.

So I watch myself.

I keep clean.

I wear wool sweaters.

If they think I'm one of them
I'm safe.

Adolph Eichman Sold Vacuum Cleaners Before the War

Imagine a well-groomed monster
at your door
lugging his wares
with the suck of small winds
in the weeds at his feet
under a green sky
with the trees smoothed over
like greased hair
his coat buttoned
about his cold heart
dreaming of the dead
front-end loaded
or bull-dozed tumbling into ditches
entwined lovers
the last shot alive
so their heads kick under blue smoke
startled sleepers
seeing the eye-level black boots walking and walking
as if they lived in basements with windows.

Imagine that ordinary monster
lugging his wares
sucking the dust

at the soles of your feet
your dead grandfather smiling
amazed and
liking him instantly.

A Second Purpose

It was there when we bought the house
the old suburban boiler
denizen of the basement living in Leave-it-to-Beaverville
lost in the back room
where we came like spelunkers
caving among wide-mouth jars
and blue fire.
I wanted it out
and wagged its weight, ah fat dancer
to the base of the stairs
called the refuse men
who came tumbling down the steps
after three strong brags
on the phone
they took one look
and with a single herniated touch
quarantined the thing and were gone swearing away
with the sound of excited hounds
cursing their own echo.
So back it went
scoring the tile on the way
with a streak of red rust like the wounded drag of blood.

Ten years passed
in the crowded furnace room
and I waited it out
until the second attempt
and my good friend Joe
said, "We can do it"
so I waggled it over
the floor fox-mouthed

with hornblende drifting down
like the shoaling of grey feathers
and we were all breathing shallow
as best as we could
Joe turning the cogs and cranks
and levers of the come-along
trussed to the jamb at the top flight
the whole house
groaning with its taut cables
an almost-going-away of caught snakes
and a no-longer slinking of chain
biting tight
where it was cinched on the boiler belly.

All day we struggled
with the whole whale weight of it
in the filthy slow walk
of its lumber
what we needed was floodwater, whirlwind
the floating of stone in storm
earth rumble, continental relocation
new mountains and a mortification of maps.
But, all night
we left it lodged halfway down
Medusa's worst work
a luckless dream's despair of sculpted dark.
I crawled above its shadow and wept myself to sleep
under the crushed ribs of heaven.

In the morning
it was easy labour at the last
and then, then
two four-tooth strangers arrived
lamenting their lives in both directions
their gums red-brown with rot
like aquifers and iron
they lifted and went
out into the agoraphobia of the city
off they clanked on a spavined truck
the underframe flinting the street

with sparks as they went and were gone
with that awful thing
of asbestos and scrap
carried to its second purpose.

Somnambulist

my son's best friend
woke up
to find himself
urinating in the bread box in the kitchen
a sleepwalk dreamer
seasoning the bread
with a salty trickle of himself
better than bed wetting, I suppose
when I used to sleep
with my soggy cousins
waking on the cold wet-mattress mornings
of our youth
to lie there all the stinking week thereafter
the tick incontinent and boggy
with the leaks of night.

Another time
he lost his first teeth
gnawing at the doorknob
of his sister's room
when she yanked it open
like a half-a-dozen toothache strings
and his teeth spilled off
like loosened pearls
enough to keep the fairy busy
flashing dimes
a dollar at a time.

And though
he's walked and mumbled
all the locks of life

he laughs at who he was
believing stories
of himself
mere words away from who he is
and who he will become
the shadow at the end of time
the one you dream
in failing light
the flavour in the bread you cannot fix
beneath the butter
the grin you see inside the smoke
you thought the door had been.

Human Wrongs

Is it wrong to bury a man beneath our lies.
To hold ourselves
in sorrowful ceremonies of heavy silence
our shoulders bent below a quiet weight
as pine boughs slouch under snow
if every soul
is crying "no! this was not he"
and he
in his box bemummed
by the yellow cloy of flower-shop grief
and a white-sand cross
adrift at the last on the arched grain
like broken time
and if the parlour threnodies
say "let the old bastard sleep"
and if the prayer
of kings and shepherds
turn to smoke
as though the little priest
were Raleigh-voiced about the stairs
behind the church
and hiding fire in his hand
instead of here

before us with his studied sadness

let daughters love cantanker
and mourn because they miss
the entire grumble of the man
lamenting even the loss of all his better faults
and let the earth contain
the smallest mar
of amber ash within the grey to mark him gone
and what will the swelled grass say?
for though I would not add
another stone to crush his chest
let's all admit
his angels were more like washing sparrows
than lonely doves.

Ballerina

Tucked in frills, her bag
pressed in stays, the ewe
makes woolly gestures
in a room of mirrors.
Her four stomachs
wallop her belly skin.
Her dainty feet
blister the planks.
She is happy only when she dances.

Coaxing beauty from her snout
her forelegs burn a perfect ring
where she spins, and her heart
grows curly nonsense.
Thrilled bleats emerge
in backward gulps.
The audience breathes
fragrant possibilities.
Should she leap,
she will never land.

Pig Roast

The evening bends close
like a secret-telling girl
and the shadows
fit their form

while a suckling turns slow on the spit
and people move in the smell
on the perfumed hill
by the house above the embered pit.

The flesh is sleek on the hog
in the heat
and the door claps once and the door claps twice
on the porch next the pool
near the field at the road
where breeze is calm as a priest
who blows a candle out.

One voice rises above the low talk
talk low as the softly mothering cluck
of hens in the dark
the voice of a ghost broken
on the wheel of life
who hung her hurt self
like a coat in the closet
alone she mourns unheard in the beer
unheard in the cutlery click and the clink of glass
unheard in the tired splash
of a single swimmer's arm
unheard in the gay sizzle
of fat in the fire
where the hog holds to the spike in his roasted mouth
like a single word sharpened
in the heart of the head.

My Father's Favourite Car

My father owned a brand new blue De Soto.
Every summer Sunday it seemed
we'd climb inside
that sun-hot automobile and wait for him to arrive
last from the house
my sister sticking to the tacky seat covers
burning her legs the same way
on the slow scald of plastic
which clung to her flesh like old fly paper
and mother
in front in her round hat and cat's-eye spectacles
and I squinting in every brilliant
direction where July caught glass
to a magnificent glare and flash
like the sudden singularity
of wet magnesium.
And then my father
with a slow sigh and a slight
left-sided sag
of a heavy man easing into the driver's seat
would enter our anticipation
and with a key click
fail to start the same goddamn
disappointing engine
which would snick, snick snick
and never roll over
and then he'd leap out and pop the hood
and look
as if he knew something which he did not
as if he understood the mystery
of black hoses and cold fire
'must be the solenoid' he'd say
and we would make
a tedious methodical egress
my mother in her low heels followed by
my sister too tall for twelve
and I
would depart for the house as well

leaving my father helpless
and half a Jonah
his body to the belt lowered into the great blue open-mawed beast
which swallowed all his hope.
And so we sojourned
every seventh day of rest
lost to an ennui of repetition
my father's favourite car
locked in that seductive stillness
like old memory
mildly recollected
when we lie to ourselves about life and its loves
and everyone hated that car
but him.

Driving South in a Dream

I was driving south
in a dream
in an otherwise fine white car
full of music, and though I was supposed to
take you with me, I simply forgot
and drifted a thousand miles alone
first crossing the border
ambassador to the rushing river
riding the heart hum of a human highway
I drove beyond the green mountains
above the sloe-berry slopes
and down the rolling length
of a hundred valleys
until I arrived
with the lowly satisfaction
of Fuller Brush
and just as my shoe toe
touched the earth
I remembered my friends
waiting in Windsor
waiting in Port McNicoll

waiting and waiting
thinking...where is he?
...where is John? and ...aren't we going together?
shouldn't he have been here by now? two days and two nights
at the window looking out, but no,
I'm deep into America...and so, I wheel about
in Birmingham and take the hot highway home
with apologies to no one
saying, "I'm late" to the wind, saying
I got lost in the starry darkness
looking past the car-map moon
at your well-lit houses
your faces pressed to the window
the breathy stencil of your worry
fogged two nostrils wide.

The Trappist Funeral

Dead Brother Ailred
lay in his box, his knees crooked up
under his winding sheet
like a storm-wrecked branch
and all his life at the last
he'd sat bent-limbed in a cruel crippled form
so death would not soften
this small mortality of bones
jointed like old boards
snapped by the weight of the world
and his face was a stone exposed
by the man-shaping light
where the stone rots back in a crag
and leaves the shaded dark wet look
half-stained.

And the trappists keep vigil
under the high arch of the chapel
where echo angels
might clap their wings in flight like silo squab

and later, eight priests praise
the summer sun come close enough
to touch the rumour of paradise
where a deep dry hole
opens in the earth to take the ache of Ailred's final slumber
while the father's mop their brows
and their faces ripen in the heat
as torpor turns them red in their robes
and I watch their watches swing past
in the tiny time it takes to pass
a stranger.

A Tale of Three Poets Locked in an Attic

Kay promised sweet Kentucky vistas
drawling out in the green delirium of the day
as she showed us the way to the four-fevered attic
her keys jangling gothic jewellery
like a wicked jailer as we heard her go
retreating from the hog's jaw
of the door clamped shut
behind us
and little we knew
we were locked in
up high in the dusty hay-mow heat
while torn moth-winged angels studied light
elsewhere, we walked the lofty compass
and looked at sun-fire tindered in the trees
where flame lines ghosted up the valley
or smeared the buildings
like smoulder drawn down the smoured edge of blood-coloured brick
and we walked Nebuchadnezzar's curse
within that furnace
above the grace of clocks
until we landed down the stairs
discovering our fate and banging the door
with the desperate flat of our hands

and we cried "Help!"
to the empty hall
"Help!" to the vacant street, "Help!"
to the sorry wind of gauzy light
that mummified us there like lamp wicks scorched
upon the webby drift of stair
that skiened our feet
where spiders ticked their needles
in a shroud for shoes

and Roger ran to break the glass above
and Marty swallowed burning darkness
in a gap of slivered light
until the cool-voiced keeper to her relief
rattled at the stillness
and we came sighing out
like fever breaking in the nearly dead
and we laughed to think
how brave we'd been
how quickly we'd confessed ourselves
betrayed our secrets, shown all the dark locations
of the soul like candles dripping tallow on a holy map
and if we're ever found again for all
within the bony rafters of that breathing beast
listen then for voices
laughing at themselves
the ashy pratfalls
our spirits make, our lives mere twists of smoke
you thought you saw.

In the Dirty Day

Through the disco doorways of Acapulco nights
I see the drunken dancers legging
as it is with the mating rituals of exotic island birds
shivering their feathers in purple light
and landing under the far cry of sea-shell stars
configured in the overspilling dark

while the music throbs
with the shock of sex
in the heat
and bodies touch together
like the bump of dumped fruit.
And the call of Klaxons
in the street
gulls above the voice
of the unloved child
who shakes a peso in a cup
because he has half the hexagon
of loser's craps for life
yearning in the bad luck of a second seven
some of us die for
in the dirty day.

And I was never young enough
my soul already mothy
within me
as a lad, I never shallowed into joy
never once felt
the superficial slip of things.
I'd rather tongue the rain
savored in the sweet damp woods
beside my father's railway fence
or steal a quiet kiss
in the scent of hay
than walk the washer's drum
of this noisy world
where everything happens at once
with the quick rucking of clothes
and the heart
like a dancer's heel
and the ache of the loins
like an egg.

The Invisible Girl

Into the beautiful Mexican daylight
when the sun swims
like bream in a blue pool
they bring their swaddled daughter
walking down the water
where we slip past
in a satin drift.
Some say she has been burned
and so the linen winding
keeps her from the hurting light.
Some say she is a child of ice
who'd melt away from sight
to the heightened hue of dampened clay.
Some say she's the spool
below the thread, unmending
when there's no spool there.
And see, her mouth moves
where puppets mum and fail to sing.
And see, her eyes blink loose
like empty fray
where the sewing's cut away.
And she is gone
with a single heavy sorrow of the heart
see how light she seems
her foot's a feather falling
where the wind-bright world
has blown.

Dark Ages

In the two great engines
of wind and water
illumine under a brilliant sun
the surf breaks roaring
in a drenched curl of foam
where a tumbled crab
snaps two exasperated hasps

111

at heaven though they will not hold
his brief career in crawling
ruined by regret
the tide to him is like a moon train
which shuttles him shallow and deep
as he is pulled against scuttling
pushed into ease and sailed sideways
like a stain upon a shifting loom
so small is he in God's esteem
even the gulls laugh crying
in the language of angels
even the fish in silver rapture
gasping on the shore, mouthing silence
with the eloquent humility
of struck children sobbing
even these compare themselves to crabs and cheer.

And I, vexed by that same tug and tumble
where waves break sundering into watery shambles
and run precisely nowhere with such purpose
as planets pretend fuming blue
under the mischief of a wizard's wand
my own more practical head
carried upon its forked anatomy
dances ankle deep in dizzy surrender
my hands open and shut, open and shut
thumb shadows fallen on palms
darken the lifeline there and trap it
like a string of chance in time.

The Night My Brain Froze Four Inches Back

I stood at a stop on a corner in Saskatoon
like a stone in winter, the street
a river
heaving an ice calf of cars
with its desire to flow
slowing to an old man's blood at my feet

while my brain
froze four inches back
in the wind
I became granite faced
shaled to a clinging white frostfall
of beard and snow-belled nostrils
a suffering Arctic dog
blinking boreal glass.
I thought of the poor.
I thought of the past
and I thought of a sharding ocean
grinding its water engines
in a sea-still catatonia
of dark-mooned night
as I stood like a halved beast
you could have knocked
spinning and marbled to bone
I'd be that hard and beautiful
hung on a hook.
I'd have gone east and lost an hour
going into that amnesia of longitude
above cloud
against sun
and seeking home
where luckless strangers sleep until they die
on benches
die in parks, die in city corners
shivering into oblivion
like the furthest stars
we cannot touch with longing
even if we dream of touching
our fingers stick like wet tongues burned
mummed to the coldest words
we speak.

The Two Chicagos

Drive past the projects in the south
their burned despair
the blacked-out scorched and empty windows
like crossword-ink forcing weird wordless silence
in the glass-checkered wall
and all the wet night moaning
through those flute holes
in tall buildings
like the bone stops
of an ancient instrument
blown by the hot and drunken breath
of cruel gods.
Drive down the jail house
clanking of her broken streets.
See how on the high wall
trains run their metal shiver
along a steely spine for the heart.
Regard how the pierced blue eye of the lake
sees only half the sky
and is fiercely blinded
by a filthy shore
its vitreous humor weeping back
to a deep response.

And now in the north
where the river drinks the lake
like a beautiful beast
with its mouth
cast wide to those western waters
and all the money of the world
trancing upward on those waves
in a thousand wild cathedrals
the white marble castles of commerce
and all the architectonics of the human planet
set in wonder
from empire and fortress
to touch the ages
stone by quarried stone

green to grey as we mused
under a purple sky
stolen from a folded rainbow in the dusk
while blue notes wailed
from a bright guitar
and all the lucky strangers
on the navy pier
spent time in silver circles
wish by wish.
 And up where the stars had dimmed
in the night refused
we might have traced
a paling horoscope
to find our lives
by place and circumstance conjoined
and cut apart
one hopeless step from home
from the coin back of a worser street
coppering down in a spin of light
to the lucky droplet
of a weighty little fortune
set lightly in the palm.

And we consider great Chicago
Sandburg's shouldering city
working in the mind
double minted
like a coin pressed twice
and seen where it is earned
and where it's spent
with the fecal river sleucing south
to Lincoln's unvexed waters
as the grand dichotomies
or our mammal souls
come clear.

Canine Pylons

When I play hockey alone with my dog
in the moonlight
I'm Gretzky flashing circles round
a canine pylon.
He's there paw-splayed
turning and scrambling
and falling
and yelping for his skated-over tail.
But when he gets it
he can really carry the puck
in his mouth
and off the pond
into the snow
where he drops it
and it makes a round slot
plunking through onto frozen earth.
A dark needle in a white haystack
acres from the ice edge.

All the 'Get it boy, get it boy,'
doesn't mean a thing.
He knows he's scored.
And somewhere
Foster Hewit has lost his voice from shouting
over barking dogs.
And somewhere Scott Young
is phoning in the scoop.
And somewhere dogs are laughing.
Somewhere that skates don't matter.
Somewhere that Wayne Gretsky
is just another pedestrian
walking four inches above the pavement.

Cartoon Cats

Flattened,
cartoon cats slither like pressed pants
down stairs
slide through door slots
sweet notes and telegrams
fall from high ledges
to be waffled
by sewer grates
or crushed by cars
hammer their paws
to throbbing
spark to a scorched frazzle
shaking hands with Niagara Falls
ride dog muzzles
in the yapping suicide of kennels
breathe feathers and
get themselves granny-knocked
till they choke up birds
confront smart alecky mice
like witless headmasters
with their hair in flames
buzz their teeth on stony nothingnesses
find themselves
hydraulicked by TNT sandwiches
suffering the quick mutations, mutilations,
transmogrifications
of the suddenly
impaled, crushed, crunched, burned,
explodes, shot, catapulted,
electrocuted, poisoned, decapitated,
sacrificing all nine lives
in the name of foolish appetite.

My Cousin Fell in Love with Archie

my cousin told me once
she fell in love with Archie
because of his red hair, because of his freckled face
because of his impish grin...
she saw herself
as the third interest
better far than the rich
Veronica Lodge, better far than blonde Betty
she'd be buxom; she be pure ink
she'd wear his letter A
burning in a branded jersey
she'd be the new girl in school
the one who'd moved to Riverdale from Canada
but never missed the snow
she'd be there, musing
beneath a thought balloon
she'd be there, scheming
in the panel, her curves drawn close
between two pyxilated jocks
she'd fall into the strip, her beauty
bleeding beyond the maladicta
of the other girls
she'd become their jealous punchlines
she'd be lost in lamps
under lightbulbs
thinking, "I'll be Archie's dream.
I'll be there in the wet of the night
when the pressmen put the paper to bed."

Thinking about Dogs at Cats

Dogs are dumb. No question.
They'll sleep slumped on stones
like an overcoat with plums in the pocket
their paws stroking
the death throes of a running dream
their eyelids flicking

they'll whimper like jilted girls
sobbing into a pillow
and chase miasmacats
to the end of chains to be jerked up short
a hundred yaps a cycle.
They eat their own regurgitant
and cock their business of cockleburs
sniff the skunk and bite the quill
with black nose brambled like a cottage whisk
then, tethered, circle the balustrade spools
on the dooryard porch till they're fang level
with the slats
and snapping at slivers
or trembling in the ratapallax of window-glass thunder,
gamboling against butterflies in the cow pasture
sliding on smelt guts in beach gravel till their coats
are sleek as a monger's slicker
thinking, 'This is a disguise!'
Thinking, 'Now the rabbit in his hill
                will mistake me for a running fish.'

But then cats were ever widdershins
and liked whoever had the sweetest milk
while dogs, heaving sighs,
their chins set on crossed paws
would die on graves
like three-day-old bouquets.

How to Put an Old Dog Down

Once upon a porch...

there was a man who had an old dog
and the dog, being old
had decided not to die
though he did nothing
but lie waiting, suffering the hours—
so the man, loving his dog
decided to put him down.

And, being kind
he considered and rejected
a litany of cruel options
for this brisk resolve—
Yes, he had decided
to dynamite his dog.

And, carrying the poor old fellow
for he could not walk
to the edge of the trees
beyond the house
he strapped the dog with TNT
so he lay like a canine car bomb
fizzing by the lit fuse.

And, the man, turning
walked towards the house
keening for his lost pet.

But Dogod was up to His old monkey business
and He revived the smitten mutt
who rose and frolicked in his fashion after his master
dragging the fuse line
like a burning lease.

And the man, being no fool
picked up his pace
as did his faithful pooch
and so on
until the fellow
hit the porch with a leap
and was overthewelcomematandintothehouse
behindthebolteddoordashingpastthekitchen
forthesanctuaryofthebackshed (breathless)   when
the hound
made the porch at a gallop
as if this were some game
half-remembered from his puppyhood
as a sudden and brutal blast
ripped through the house

sending shock waves
rippling across the field
and bringing shingles, and bits of dog
twisting down through the tree tops
the dog's nose intact
still snapping at squirrel smells
while it fell.

Dogs and Horses

These are the days of dogs and horses.
These are the days
of fallow, the countryside
exotic with weeds
and empty barns.

The sheep are pretty without dung.
Their newborn lambs
no longer the colour of cotton dipped in iodine
for the dressing of wounds.

All the gentrified artists are harmlessly happy
and working their trade
in milk paint and cloth
and the cows moo politely from quilts
above the swishing pails
as white as Queen's linen
and the pasture's unflappable
as Elizabeth at chapel—oh

the dogs stay beside the fire
like folds in paper
and pigs are deep in thought
philosophers on the verge
of great ideas

and horses jump and canter
like a carousel

because all the best animals
have poles in their heads
and if they move then
out of their stagy circles
let them move like Greek statues
bumped against politely in galleries
or tapestries stirred
by a breeze along a summer wall.

My Dog Barks at a Remax Hot Air Balloon
It was summer all day
and the sky
held every planet blue.
The pool was warm and quiet
so the water trickling back
from each standing swimmer's arm
was less than the sum
of a single sip.
And each of our pasts
mere damp-shadow shrinking
on the green sweep
of a love-lit life
where we were pegged by time
as if in the slow steeplechase of a cribbage hour.
We moved half-steps like grazing moose
waders unworried by all the wars in the west
unworried by the poor
and the drunken
sleeps of those sad to be other than ourselves.
We dragged our elbows
like milk skimmers
in the shallow trace
where fallen flies were merely frantic
an instant
before the final futile buzz
of being black and fatal and wet
as small Ophelia fairies drowned and despairing of the sky.
And even the dog

lay tossed on the yellow stone of her belly
until with a helium hiss
the hot air balloon came floating over the trees
in a misdirected journey
from a century before
its shadow like disappearing ink darkening the grass
in random circles
with a brief poisoning of light.

The dog saw
hackled up her hair
and barked her watch
with that thief-catcher's enthusiasm
she spared for postmen and the paper girl.
She bit the air
and jumped
as if she might catch
and haul it down, the large blue bloat
withering flat
deflating like a wet windless parachute.
And it was clear
she meant to harm the humans
in the sky
to bring that Brobdingnagian fruit basket
full of fellows
tumbling down and thumping the earth
like apple pickers
falling through an orchard
in the clouds, saying with each subsequent bark
"Step off the wind, stranger
and sell me a house in heaven."

One Scorched Glove On a Beach*

for John Oughton

I woke from a dream
and heard these lines within

"at the end of the day
 the shadows fall like soot
 and nothing is left of happiness"

and I wonder
when did the world go mad?

I think of my friend
flying lost above the lake
in a lightning flash
and all that was found of him after
was a floating cushion
and a bobbing cap.
I think of my friend
dying in the morning
his heart going slow under his hand
like the swearing of an oath.

I think of the tumble of numbers
at the end of an age
like the rolling over
of an automobile odometre
and I, not yet fifty
remember the boy who became the man
imaginary
and see what the mirror portends
in the bone lines under the beard
and the temples' greying pulm
and know that it is good
that I do not see so well
into glass
and the lad beneath the life
though Dorian to an old soul
has one or two enthusiasms left

to play out
if the money lasts.

all that was found after the Challenger exploded was one scorched glove on the beach

The Pig Dance Dreams

The man who dreamed
a pig
dancing on his chest
leaving pronged trotter marks
in the flesh
dancing to wrestle
his jowl
against a human cheek
pig saliva sudsing
at his ear
dampening his hair so it clung
to the straw tick
wondered
if God loved him enough
to send this lean razorback.
Every night
he came like a lover
to grapple and wear the man out
dancing on his ribs
poking him in the belly
snorting at his nostrils
hot pig breath
winding like a fetid river
into his lungs
until he was startled awake
clawing up
from sleep like a bird
in a chimney flue
to find no pig
but his hands smelled of swine

and his ears were tender screams
of swine
and his arms were bristling
angry with spiked hair of swine
and his mouth
had the taste of raw swine
his tongue lathered
with his own mad speech
his own fear
pushed against his teeth
so they ached like the ribs of a cage
holding in some
live animal with the urge to rend
explode a prayer
along his jaw
"God! Take away this pig."
so he fell
into pigless sleep
tame sleep lucid sleep with no room
for darkness
just a thin light always on
docile and cold as a fridge light
when you opencloseopencloseopenclose
the large white door.

Not to Lie Back Beneath the Heavy Engine
of the Stars And Let the Heavens Fall

poem after a plane disaster in India

This pain is too much whisky in the water.
Too much
for the casserole consolations
of neighbours meaning well.
There are no words
nor silences sufficient
nor bishops wise enough
in all the wide horizons
and deeper waters

of the darkest nights
where moonlight breaks its bones
among white birches
and the fragile webs of snow
weft like torn dream catchers
left overlong in the wind
where the cruel-to-foxes cold
crawls in fractures over stone.
We give our hearts to loss
and breathe beneath the frost
but when we bear children
we bear them to outlive us.
To love us well
and grieve us dying.
Not to lie back beneath the heavy engine of the stars
and let the heavens fall.

Oh What a Wonderful Wind

The starling with one dead winter leaf
stuck on his foot
walks in my yard
like a fly-paper comic
and he
yaws his one leg wide
refusing to be crippled
by the ridiculous.

This existential moment
the sense of himself
suddenly larger on the right
gets him to speculating as to why
his birdness has been
transmogrified to include
the tree, as if
God were a zany cartoonist
with one daffy shoe
too big to be worn

to the creation dance.
And then, because he cannot strut
our starling flies, the startled leaf
thinking,
"oh, what a wonderful wind!"

The Day I Found Four Score of Starlings Dead in the Franklin

The day I found four score of starlings
dead in the Franklin
the living room smelled
like a pigeon coop.
We'd been away for the summer
and they'd flown
down the flue
and been trapped there
beating their black wings blacker against creosote
then finally falling to form a heap
the bottom birds crushed and stiff, long dead
each one flat like a crushed corsage.
The top birds
some still warm, still full of what it meant to fly
to hold the sky
beneath them like a nest.

And afterwards I climbed the house
to fix a wire grill
above the hole
while the starlings circled anxiously
as if I were sealing off
their last passage of escape.
As if the chimney were a tunnel
they'd dug
to get out of the world.

My Alibi for an Eventful Wednesday in May

I am lost in a room
where we did not meet
listening to the song
that isn't ours
thinking the thoughts
I didn't think
when we didn't meet here.
I don't remember
what you didn't wear then.
I think
it wasn't pink.
I don't recall
what you didn't
whisper in my ear.
I think it wasn't spring
when we weren't here.
I don't remember
not kissing you
after we didn't drink
champagne.
All that I recall
is that the nude
who didn't dance
on the table
wasn't you.
            spring 1970

First Love

At sixteen
my first love
snorted speed.
Shot blue dots
in her arms
so thin
the needle nicked the bone.

My first love
dreamed that the touch
between her legs
was an injection.

Her eyes
wiggled
in bony sockets
sniffing the white powder
through the shaft of a pen
as if she were holding a fragrant rose.

My first love
bloomed
like a drinking glass
dropped on a tile floor.

A hard girl
shivering
in short sleeves
her soft eyes begging
when I'm broken
will you fix me
will you fix me
will you fix me
asshole.

Somewhere in this Poem I Wanted to Tell You I am Ashamed of My Own Nakedness But I Couldn't Figure Out How

He tells me they skinny dip
whenever they can

and I imagine them
he and his wife
waist deep in the still moonlit waters
of Meldrum Bay

like the upper half
of perfect human sculptures
set upon a gallery floor.

The delicate light
on her cool uplifted nipples
his forearms
skimming the surface
leaving a simple heartbreaking crease
in his wake
the small fish schooling
at their calves
making curious nips
like the mouths of lovers.

Free as children.
Free as ancestral hunters.
They walk, slow dream walkers
in the timeless loop of soothing weightlessness

and then he dives
his footheels a small rounded moment
disappearing in the spilled ink
of the bay.

 She stands alone now
in the consequence of his motion
that pulses tenderly against her ribs.

For a Woman Gone One Hundred

She has outlived the pennies of her birth
and seen her childhood postage
grown more precious
for all the dead-letter nations
disappearing into the larger mails of maps
and measured her ages
by the death of kings
their brief assumptions of the throne

mere summers crowned in flowers.
And her loss of friends
as many as the graves of war
and she the last to know
the suffering of elms
and she the girl of horses
become a woman of the moon
with her sisters
at walk   about the stars
her daughter's daughters dreams
the same as son's.
And she, doyen of all remaining days
shakes time like a stone
to see the dowager, the parlour dowsabel
and all the other scolds of earth
in the closing up of ghosts.

The drizzle on a window pane at night
could never grieve enough
to name them all
nor the heart count in its dark house
the bitterly quieted loves.

Onions, A Love Poem Based on a True Story

I walked in.
The house smelled of onions.
The cook book lay open, spine down
dog-eared on pages
marked, "Onion"
and beside the table
lay the empty orange mesh bag
littered with scraps of orangish onion skin
curled like peeled sunburn
warning of the meal to come.

Not to be ungrateful,
for Cathy seemed pleased to have accomplished
this crazy repast,

first I dug my spoon beneath the crusty cheese
and sipped the deliciously decocted soup.
And then tied into the next spicy onion course, and then the next,
the next, the next, and so on
until I had consumed more onions
in that brief hour
than my onion-eating uncle would eat
in a week of eating salted Spanish onions sliced on white bread.
That night I lay in bed
my heart burning like a wet magazine
and began belching
the backwards smell of anaesthetic
counting onions jumping fences under an onion moon
dreaming of Cathy reading air mail with tears in her eyes.

I Want to Be the Poet of Your Kneecaps

I want to be a poet
of your kneecaps
to call them out
like an archaeologist
gently brushing earth from a curve
of painted crockery
a thousand year old preciousness
he might hold in his palm
saying, this is the reason I am
alive, I exist to rescue
the ages residing at your bending legs.

I want to be the poet
of your ankles
those rosebuds closed above your feet
on either side
to say
there is a promise blooming
in the bone
a sweetheart's secret pressed forever
in that book of flesh.

I would be
the poet of the nape of your neck.
I would be the poet
of toes.
I would linger
musing on the neat fiveness
of your hands
the tiny divot of your philtrum
the creases of your ears.
Surely the blueness of your iris
is pool enough for some,
but what of the pupil
black as a circle of felt
on a false poppy.

Yes, there are certain obvious
flowers of longing
but I would be the poet
of difficult desire
let me celebrate
the slight plumpness of the belly
about the navel
let me be the words
connecting your luminous cable
to the stars.

Poem Based on a Conversation with a Black-eyed Goalie in a Hockey Dressing Room

He is her live-in boyfriend.
Last week she'd hit him
in the face with a pan
and so Frank says
"the flap jacks
resembled him the next day"
and I imagine them
peeled up by spatulas like wheat-flour death masks.
And this week

she'd punched him twice
in the eye...
his theory, "she's testing
to find out whether I'll be abusive"
meaning: will he ever hit back
and although he laughs
he means every word
and I imagine
a magazine list:
"Ten things to try if you suspect
your new boyfriend
might be a hitter"
a Chatelaine quiz involving
when to use knives
involving, the smoking gun as a last resort
the burning pillow
the small dark pin-feathered hole in a sleeper's head
where he dreams one silver bullet
and he seems so peaceful
when he's dead
and "he never struck me once,"
she said.
"Not even when I stabbed him
in the night.
He must have really loved me."

Little wonder
that he cringes for a kiss.
And they're "thinking of having kids
                together."

Years later, all his children resemble rumpled skillets
and he's the proud father
saying, "the night you were conceived, boys
                I didn't see it coming"
as he shows his sons
the slight relief of his skull repeated
as a warning
in a gallery of pans.

Never Buy Too Much Life Insurance

you'll tempt your wives to greedy grief
invite the widow in
wearing weeds
weeping away the black week
with one wet eye on the money
you'll murder yourself
in perpetuity
the bank notes fluttering after
tickering down
like a lovely moonlit snow
much sad singing "quelle domage
il nege, it snows"
you'll dig yourself a golden grave
see how the coin
comes shivering down
how sunlight molts like a sick fish
and me with my two-penny eyes
a cheapskate's poker ante
one coppery blink away from forever.

Know this
I love you
even to the very Hitchcock music
sawing at the door
even to the dark wing
ravening at the window
even to the very knives and poisons
of your secret heart
see how I sign
and freely purchase one future
one long and seamless cruise
without me.

You Weren't Here When You Were Away

My wife says this
by the pool in the summer upon my return
for I was away
within the unfixed image of myself
in the south
where heat annealed the colour
brightly on the hills
by daylight seared like fire
looked at through a burning glass
and yes
I was away in the solipsism
of absence
yes, I was away
in the centuries of memory
and map inches
measured beyond the third unfold
but I thought on you
love
and I appeared beside you
where the pillow dipped
with a blink of linen
and I touched you there
with a water drop of dream's caress
that would not wake desire
though it close the stars
together whispering sparks
in an intimate astronomy
the night sky shares its galaxies
caught burning while you slept.

Paying Attention

The Half-Way Tree

The half-way tree divides the walk
between the house that's gone
and the school no longer there
and this, the corner
of the church that was
and this, the windmill strut
upswept that held a disappearing blur
propelling water from the earth
and as we drive the squared mile
through the blink of Mull
and past the neighbours lost
where old dogs mourned their lonely names
within grey barns
and down the gravel shoulders ditch by ditch
in a trail of smoke we come
two smokes long
my mother's memory
could build an elm
into a shade so large
it held cool service
on the orchard grass
a stain too deep for sunlight
to remove
in its scouring round a stony clock
and there my aunt would stray
meandering home among the cows
and of the fifty country lads and girls
beneath the bell
some thirty mothers
aging in the gong
some twenty fathers
living in the knell
and beyond the toll of morning
as we move

the ancient elm
that warmed a winter when it fell
has cast its scattered leaves about the air
and sunk to nothing in the snow
but that brief fire
in a child
lights a way to life
and if you lean against that ghost of wood
you shake tall branches
and send blank birds away
to the wind in wisps of how it was.

Thinking Like Children

My father used to ask a question:
riddle me this—
two snakes are
eating each other tail first, what happens?
and I imagine
a shrinking circle
ending as a blink
like the sudden disappearance
of a pricked soap bubble
and they are gone—erased
like a smudged vowel
gone like the inner radiance of rain
from still water
a smoke ring hazing away to nothing
though it began as grey halo
on a dust angel
my six-year-old sister, musing on the meaning of life
when I was four, wondering aloud in the ellipsis...are we a dream
being dreamed
and if so, what if the sleeper
wakes, and I think of myself in the mind of a startled god
and we cannot hold our shape long
in the event of the blue day become
thin water colour

washing down wet paper
and I cannot answer
though I sleep, often.
And now, my children grow into themselves
as with the last breath inflation
of an adult life
they fill their clothing
and seem real enough.

And I look at the world they enter
where they live at the centre of our concern
and I name the one snake
Future, and the other
Here and Now
and am careful of their appetite
for memory and dream.

Deepening Time*

I am looking through a window at night
out into the darkness
and I see myself
as one might see
a photograph behind a glass
in brilliant light.

I am looking
into deep water
at my own face
like a floating lily
with the back of my head
to the sky
and the stones below the sky
where fish kiss hunger
and wave their drowning veils.

And I see
the shallowing of strangers

walking past
their watches measured voices
marking time

and I touch
the emerald river
by the whirlpool
where it flows
between the limestone walls
like a serpent
sliding by
and I dip my hand
below the foam and green
my fingers disappear
and like a handless statue
I am holding nothing
swallowed to the wrist in silky light
that roams
among the stars of dust and mist arriving here
and I wonder
at the focus of a mind awake
how clear the blue must come
before we look becoming blue

how like a painting
not quite there we are
if ten-thousand-year-old rivers
show us nothing
and slate is blank
against a tiny life
while swallow tails
drink purple nectar in the sweet vervane
and flex their velvet hinges
like an absent door.

*time deepening is an expression coined to describe the habit of certain people who
would make their lives count for more by engaging in several simultaneous experi-
ences such as listening to an audio book, going for a simulated bike ride in the
woods, answering a cell phone, and taking in nature through the window while
they sort their mail and make supper.*

I Too Can Show the Way

Where would you lead me friend?
into what future
and from what past
and by what light guide
and for what purpose go
and to what end
and with what faith...
for if I follow
where the hills are hard
and if I cross cruel rivers
on the way
stepping stone by stone
between the foams and froths
that break the water's voice
and if I look to see
who comes behind
by my example then
we share a path
and breathe to climb
and step against the slope
to see the valley's hard green ease
beyond a blind horizon's call
and if you'd named the dangers
one by one
and sent those glories free before
how then
to temper knowing
if I do not touch the stones the rivers touch
how then to look upon the map
and say
see there, we went together
      I too can show
the way.

One by One

One by one my friends are entering
other lives.
Some venture
so far away we need five maps
to plot their absence
and a twelve-tongue journey
to follow their flight
over the blank blue
drowning out of voices
and though there are a dozen weathers
between us
a score of storms
and quiet rains we cannot hear
and though they live
where night-crossed faces sleep
while we are working
we are both sun and moon
both satellite
and stillness
both image and source
for living on and of the earth
we travel through each other's lives
lighting our way ahead
with love
to leave a little shade behind
by going.

There is Something Submerged

There is an altitude
beneath landscape. A way of living
under snow.
A river flowing under ice.
Listen. You might hear the bumping heads
of those
not quite drowned.

Watch the shifting surface of the fields
for stone
heaved by frost.
Record the slow hearts of frozen frogs.
The blip of their cardiograms
like something melting
in your garden
filled with the relaxing shapes of pumpkins gone to mould.
And if the grave of your old dog
begins to breathe
remember how he used to lie at night
running in his sleep
how he swam in the shallow water strongly stroking his paws,
he does not know how far he has to go
to touch the earth.

The Whistler Swans in My Father's Fields

This spring
they'd landed there in the thousands
with the snow that lay
where it falls
or melts a little
against the black
and darkens the seeping soil
black till
white swans
calling themselves down
like the far cry of children
playing behind buildings
in the closed echo
of some inner square.

And they stay a week
and then a second
the way grandmothers keep lonely vigil
in daughter's kitchens
the tea kettle whistling

two half steps from the table
the rain
catching against the window
like a soft-clawed cat
climbing glass
saying "how is it I can't reach the world
I'm looking at?
Why is it I can't touch
into and through this invisible stillness
to the action beyond?"
And then Jan and I
are driving west of Aylmer
where the hawks outdistance
their own expectations of flight
by gliding
like the feathered silence
that comes on the verge of sleep...
that same kind of slow passage
the trees manage at dusk
or the slip of tide
shushing down pebbles and shells
until they're still
and settled the way gravity
wishes it were

and she says
"in the woods
you can smell the deer"
and she means
more than musk and scat
more like oak in wine
seasoned in wood.
And I say, "yes"
I can scent them
beyond the radio light
and ashy smell
in the cramped chrysalis of cars.
It's something like
having an ear on your chin
and owling for the movement of mice.

Something like stroking the moon
with your back
and seeing your shadow shape
shutter the entire thirty miles
across the lake.

Hide the Button

In my grandmother's winter kitchen
where it was always warmest by the cast-iron stove
we played hide the button
though I did not imagine
how a coat unclosed
or trousers dropped
where the thread had lost its hold
left behind in the waist cloth like blue sutures
how a tired father
might sag through his shirt
where the belly showed
or a lover
might wish away blouse buttons next the bodice hasp
with nervous hands
nor the loneliness of button holes
nor the chilly longjohn gap
where the wind gets in
and by all the round blue beauties
we hid like doll's eyes gone blind under day beds
by all the yellow coins
we gathered into one gold purchase
by all the buttons black-as-cough-drops
for soothing the voice of uncles
by all the tiny red
and incandescent button hearts we found
and held to our breasts like fencing wounds
with my cousins shouting
"warm! warm!...you're burning up!"

and I
come loose like child's mending
in that heat, become the button's second purpose
and run the length of thread
from where it's licked
to where it meets the eye.

In the Harmonious Kitchens of Christmas

In the harmonious kitchens of Christmas
womb-warm with what ovens do
and alive with the talk of women
smoothly rippled like coffee cream in the air
one aunt romancing the turkey with a spoon
of its own juices
another stirring gravy on the stove top
a third is looking through cupboards
for spices, doors opening and shutting
like the Marx brothers in a hotel hallway
while mother unstructures the squeaky footstool
and climbs to hand down drinking glasses enough
teetering from the comfortable vertigo of the top shelf
one, two, three, four, five, six, seven, etc.
turned over as if to listen to secrets through tables
huge stethoscopes for the heartbeat of footfalls
or conches for the bloodrush of an inner sea.

Is it nostalgia to remember
how they stood in the perfume of what they cooked
extolling the virtues of aprons
and telling the domestic biographies
of those they loved most
clapping their quilted oven mitts
and rocking on their heels with whipped potatoes
billowing in the pan as if they carried clouds.

In the complicated dance step of preparing a meal
clutching cutlery to their breasts

like dangerous silver bouquets
answering the chime of something done
believing the huge irresistible comedy of the day
while in the sweet rum-coloured sunlight of the cold landing
they click with food
pleased by the comforting insanity of the final rush
for the table
or the afterfull sudsing hubbub of dishes
with uncles so stuffed
they sit patting their bellies like split-seam pillows
half expecting feathers to puff out
between shirt buttons.
Fat men plucking their wattles
and talking of horses.

Tonight when the house is quiet
it will remember nothing.
The bones will settle together in the trash
the gravy congeal in the cool pantry pot
and the table scraps will amuse the country dogs
avoiding sleep long enough
to smack them down
stealing a poultry thigh and
beating their jaws like pruning shears
on a tough branch.
And snow might fall in moonlight
like angels coming back from holidays.
While God is somewhere
putting the kettle on
for all the women who have ever lived.

As Long as It Isn't Sweet

"As long as it isn't sweet"
my dear old blind grandmother says of her hospital food
repeating it like an incantation
against fruits and cakes.
A curse against confection
and the sugary jams
that ooze with strawberry hearts

148

in the centre of jars.

"As long as it isn't sweet"
she chants
a prayer response.
"As long as it isn't sweet"
her tongue rejecting
such honeys and candies and creams
insulting the cherry in its juice
the disused nectar drips
until it grows monotonous in sticky pools.

"As long as it isn't sweet
          as long as it isn't sweet
            as long as it isn't sweet"

As if we conspired with spoons
against her wishes.
As if we haunted her with peaches
plump and lit from within their skins
like gold and crimson lamp shades.
As if we hung about with figs on our fingers
and gum drops bumping together in wrinkled bags
waiting to cloy her
like a fat little girl
with buttery lickings from the beater bowl
so she ached in the night
and quickened her step in dreams
against desire.
But for now she takes her little sips
of bitter tea
and I weep in the shallowing foreground
to see how much the darkness has taken
her trust.

The Dream Picnic of Rondeau Bay

At the dream picnic of Rondeau Bay
the table is long
and laid with food.
The cherries are sweet and latticed with crust.
The tarts are plump with jam
and the angel cake has portions enough for all.

The swing set shifts
with the easy pump of bending legs
and the see saw
rises and falls on fulcrums like the balance
of feathers and gold.

And some seek shade of maple
shade of larch.
And some the cool and rolling lake.
And some the smooth warm bay.
And some a game of catch
the sure and easy arc of the ball
the certain spin of the stitch
and the dying kinetic heft
as it pulls a hand back
to break a fall
with mothers on tandems
and cousins at golf.

Out far where the grass is thin with walking
or in close
where it is groomed for sleep
or in the sand
dry sprigged so it pokes and bends
like wire fine enough
to fasten dainty shells
I see the ghosts of those we've lost...
 handsome Allan
rounding the bases once
like a watch set an hour wrong
and laughing because the ball has taken flight
forever

and gentle uncle Tom
the sweet American, tanned and tall
the soft assurance of his voice
his heartbeat touching air
 and grandfather Harry resting in the glow of children
 and grandmother Lila
keeping her faith with the land
in the look of flowers
under a sky as blue as morning glories
blooming in her hair
where the sun has dropped its traces
and sits still as a study lamp
that leaves its amber circle
on an empty chair
 and all the curving clockwork
of what was occurs remembered real.
I feel the pulse above the hand
and say what's true in time
is true for always
even as far as the stars invisible
beyond the stars I see.

The Art of Walking Backwards

You thought you understood
the art of walking backwards.

The way the ground turns to air
at the cliff edge.

The way stones feel
against the heel.

The way the rock face
might slam the spine against a jut.

The way window glass
shatters around you
in a dangerous puzzle of cutting reflections.

The way the door stays in its joists
or a tree clings shivering to its roots.

The way thin ice gives over deep water
or the swamp sucks you in slowly
like a dropped stone.

One more step
and you will be beyond the verge
free falling
with gulls in the canyon.

There Are Certain Days When Shaving Seems Like Suicide

I remember admiring my father's face
after each close Sunday shave
his adult throat
suffering the slits and slashes
of that outrageous morning's new blade
the sink water thinly juiced
with his slow-plitting essence
where cut hairs blinked and gathered
against the small skull islands of shaving soap
how he occasionally mended these nicks
with little bits of toilet tissue
epoxied to the flesh
by crimson clots
though one or two would drop
like rain-wet geranium petals
or later when he would peel them
from his gullet
above the collar of his crisp white shirt
how he would well again
from the unstypticed wound
the tiniest pool of red
like an ink blot on a valentine heart
to which he would apply a Kleenex corner

but if he forgot them
these rosy rags would ride his larynx
raised in church song
till my mother nursed them from their station
like precious overseas postage stamps
careful not to re-excite the bleeding place.
Instead of God
I might sit and contemplate these
tiny puckered blossoms
where my mother set them on the pew
beside my sister's white communion gloves
stigmata on the blonde grain of the wood
the despair of flowers
fallen from the brief season of my young father's grief.

My Old Dog Died in My Arms

I felt him go loose
and he slid
from the sweet domestic circle
of my embrace
his eyes
empty as pools of tea-brown ink

and I could hear a suffering October window
grieving rain
as if it cared

I sensed him   slacking
and was surprised by how light and frail he seemed
how like a balsa thing
weary as a slanting cone of dry beach sand
drifting into a hollow
ribbed with sticks
he slipped
and was no more.

I will bear the burden of my kindness
at the end
and find it hard
to love this dreary world
this morning
weeping, this October mourning
when my heart weighs broken
like the thread that kept these water droplets
from tracing gravity to its source
in the glass.

The Unforgiven Father

A fragile robin blinks in my hand
a bird my son has found
broken-winged, crush-footed
listing in the cottage grass
its fledged breast speckled like a freckled cheek
living out the afternoon in fear of cats.
I feel the gentle rise and fall
of its final feathered breath
and the crooked strike of its feckless foot
against my palm
while the robin rocks its head to fend off death
in the elderberry radius of its terrified eye.
I must seem some huge cruel beast
and so I snap its neck
and lay him out upon the earth
like a tie against a jacket.

My boy, who thought to save him
for half the fatal day
by thrusting crumbs and gritty worms
at his hooked beak
had wreathed a nest and cobbled up
a crooked fence cocked against intrusion
then guarded the perimeter
and watched him fade

like a sleepy reader
for the hours left him coining one by one
like pennies counted out
to hold a dollar at one hundred.

Now he sobs behind a wall
where he declares his sadness
for the poor swell
that sags in a simple lump
while I gnaw a little grave
with a spade
my foot upon the heel
I double gravity
and make a way forgiveness cannot find
my own heart
like a muffled knuckle
softly rapping at a bedroom's private door.

Funny Violence and Cartoon Dreams

I want to say to my sons"
"...if you promise to imagine,
           I'll promise to remember..."
But false memory
and desultory dreams
intervene

and I become
the raging curmudgeon
mistaking fashion for disrespect
and you become
the slouches I fear
loose with language
acting at life
as if every sidewalk were a stage
and all the sideshow video clowns
were paradigms to print your coins
and palm your faces.

And it gets to be about
haircuts, somehow.
And it gets to be about
trousers and hats
and the sartorial wars
that divide father from child
and the two-legged tipping of dining room chairs
seems important.
And because I long to save you
from the funny violence
and cartoon dreams
of a culture gone mad
never mind
my fuzzy afro that used to fill a door
never mind
the danger in the wilds of being young
I've learned something
and I want you to ignore
the way I learned it.
I've salvaged some truths
from the rubble of experience.
No need to repeat my mistakes my sons.
Believe me
even as you
move into the world
like two small fragile boats
leaving the still stream
casting your paddles
into the open waters of this shared sun-bright lake.

Hockey Heart

His hockey heart
beats alone in the air
the surest player
on a pond of dreams
a boy
one skate boot on the bench

one on the foot
his fingers stiff
blowing his brittle hands
to get the frost out of the joints
always the last to leave
reliving the game, lost or won,
curing his mistakes
thinking of tomorrow
as if it were already yesterday
knowing that everything happens twice
once in the present
and once in the past.

Sinkers

for two boys drowned in Port Stanley, June 1998

The lake leapt up at the end of the pier
and licked him from his feet
like the sticky tongue
of a huge insatiable beast
and he was nearly seventeen
and stupid to the storm
which was ravenous
and rolled him of his soul
loud as stone rumble
his body tumbling in the underwash
the skein of his bone
latheing out
a crone slubber of dead wool
unwound from the sheep foam of his last breathing
wild weather
sumping the pier-hollows
where on better days
boys had sat on the roof slope
of concrete
casting in the calm
where their hooks plooped
like the final fatal skip a pebble takes

before it drops in the deep
where fish live
and the lines hung
like drowned marionettes dancing
a dance of veils
where the green gods
wave their weedy hair
and think .

And his friend saw him go
and leapt in after
where the blind wash swilled
and he was the second lad lost
that day
as the hero chases the fool
while boats bumped together
jumping on their harbour ropes
and wise captains watched the rough rain
rising backwards
where the breakers slapped their tails
these two doomed boys entered a second illusion
while coffin makers hammered cold homes.

Perhaps the younger boy
had stood bubbling baby talk
in the yo-yo of his mother's harness years before
perhaps he'd lain
in his father's open arms
mocking love by lolling there
perhaps he'd dangled his legs
into the danger beyond his bed
where the water-bright linoleum
of his own blue room
swallowed life.
Perhaps he'd awoken that very day
planning the evening
and the day after
regarding the dog-eared calendar
to measure the lapse till summer

and as I remember
riding the bus to the Rodney pool
as a boy
and being called sinker
by the girls
while we splashed
in the cold shallows
like minnow tubs full of silver sunlit fins
and then stood shivering on the deck
in the skinny shock of wet light and July breathing
we were pale
and didn't think of dying
our arms out and stiff
as laundry starched by summer
and I became tadpole
the second season
following the guide rope
out where my feet slipped
and caught the weird half-gravity
of water
while those life guards
shrilled their whistles
like cruel birds

and I thought of the boy
I was, watching the lake
later, seeing Erie Eau
seeing Port Stanley, seeing Dover
seeing Dicky Lowell's drowned father
pulled fat as a fish
from his first grave
and I see those two boys
suddenly disappearing from the end of the pier
battered lifeless
and dumb as waterlogged wood
their deaths sinking
in the wintering hearts of their fathers
like the long cold adrenal needle
of a gorgon's gaze.

Bread Is a Living Thing

She speaks of bread
as a living thing
and if you listen
you can hear
how bread breathes alive
how wet dough
feels in the hands
as it rolls and stretches and lolls
a tacky interacting creature
undulating as in a sensual sea
and oh, the yeasty way of it
how they have built
an oven in the square
a wood-fire gathering place
where women come and men as well
with their weighty sours
wrapped and newly born
to the touch
as it is with the sun on the field
and the rain in the yard
when water-barrel lilies
float in liquid light
and good darkness
goes down deep between the staves and bands
holding in warmth
as it rounds a room at home
and why are we not all
drawn there by lodestone-
love and care-filled conversation

even in the unending blur
of a city blizzard
they come down
to this olfactory oven
with their work in their hands
under tea towels, wanting as they do
to tell us true stories to sleep by.

The Dog Who Died in the Dark

The darkness does not fall, rather
it rises from the land
through half-completed sky
beyond where Brian's barn
is clucking with the slow
and percolating settling down of hens
whose yellow beaks go dim
and peck the planks
like rain that cannot quite arrive
at gathering
and then they vent their eggs
completely grey
in filthy ovals
wobbled into straw
as warm as lamp bulbs
dimmed in rooms
too dark to read.
And from this black-leafed garden
from this fire-haloed yard
the dog went out
to lope along a wend of road
and struck a thump of chrome
a sudden weight of self
within himself
he could not lift
though he'd been blind with joy
till then
and someone found him gone
beyond his call
beyond the low echo of his name
within the sorrow of a voice alone.
A ditch stone
gritty with the work of spring
might have more life
set on a hill
red granite shining wet
and still
he would be evermore

the dog who died in the dark
letting the darkness down
as it is with
the unhitching of an open web
a wafting
and the light outside
pushing where the darkness goes.

Bombay the Labrador

Bombay the Labrador is a big black buckle-high boy
who runs his head
nodding under the breakfast table
as board by board
each coffee cup
clinks its spoon
like a ghost with a sweet tooth
and then he knocks
his flat skull
palm to palm
looking for praise
after he's shambled past playing tail-duster
with knickknacks
like an argument in a jewelry shop.
And he's one rainy musky dog's length
outside chasing a stick's conclusion
in the wind or on the water
even dashing into cold October lakes
his legs like two boys running
the hind lad, just a little faster
than the front
he comes back stumbling slightly sideways
like laughter echoes crossing
voices into joy.

A Taxi Driver Tells Me Johnny Weissmuller Died at Home in Acapulco Nine Years Ago

I sit in the sun
on diamond beach
near Acapulco, Mexico
and watch bird shadows shrink
as back on black
the living feathers join the land
and if they fly up and up
the shadows grow
like water thrown to cool the sand
by splashes from the market steps
until they disappear
beyond the dampened light.
But souls are shadowless
in flight
and so the swimmer
whispered off the heights
as forever young in film
he wrestled with the river crocs
those dying reptiles bubbled under by his strength.
Yet on a wall of photographs
he lives and smiles
half naked, modest in his paradise of palms
and I remember Windsor Sundays
when he visited our house
as Lord of Apes immortal and love wise
broken hearted at the loss of beauty
in an English stranger's mind
so language simple in his sadness
he could have saved
the planet from colonial wars
that burned on maps
he'd never seen
scorching nations he'd never known
the fire's border red and black.
But who can understand
the loss of strength that comes with age
like Samson shorn in sleep

my father's own fardel of years
the bending bones of women
the branches of their spines
peach-heavy with a quarter life to live
as if to read the road below themselves
for the drop of crooked shadows there.
 And nine years since
his cry went jumping up
in echoes on the wind
to wake the lions at the gate
the yawning golden cats
or further off
black panther's blink
green sentience in trees of night
indifferent to the lack of light. Meanwhile
Orion slips his belt and drops his sword
and the dipper spills a coal-black milk
 tarring down in darkness on a starless sky.

Reading the River

I look at the water line
on your door jamb in London
and see in the dark
a disbelieving stain like the height mark
a mother might have made
to measure her child in the morning
fifty years ago
and think of you
walking wet to the heart
like the wading of roses in shadow
in that old season of Pharaoh's weather
watching the deluvial rise
or your own ruin
in the floating by of chairs
and the flowing past of cloudfall
and the staying still of mirror trees
anchored deep below themselves.

Meanwhile the swimming carp
kissed half the glass
you used to lift to let the day
breathe in
and stir the curtain skirts
like angel-fish fins
or the broad green leaves of weeds in water
and in the curious aquarium
of a sunken house
they navigate above the bed
like visions of drowning dreamers
and in the less than perfect summer
after, crossing your mud-rugged lawns
walking home
through the silting down of memory
into the thief shambles
of your life settling back like a sinking boat.
 I think of Walter
reading the rapids
on the Coppermine for signs of stone
and threading his craft
north in the rough beauty
where death steals time
like the simple picking open
of a pocket watch.
I think of Bible Egypt
drifting on lazy rhythms
in the fertile ages of empire
cresting in the alchemy of noon.
I think of the Grand
in Caledonia
and the Speed in Guelph
and the unvexed Father of Waters
 sorrowing south
to name the dead
where they have disembogued into the salty Gulf.

And I think
of the wind in a rocking chair

like a ghost
that watches the street
as boys watch branches
slipping under bridges
town by town
until the Thames behind my Uncle's farm
received the willows
at the bend
like the sad and careful wading in of women
deciding about love.

Abandoned Mill

We climb down beside the frozen waterfall
marbled white and yellow
like the beard of an ancient god
touching down the slope
below the cold cataract to behold
where water trickles free
from the ice at our feet.
To hear the hollow sound of its falling
we place our ears to that rising wall
like doctors to the chest of the dead.
This is the echo of rain
the voice of the stream
straining to speak
what with the mill wheels seized by rust
and the fallen wrights tangled among
dogwood and staghorn roots
the stone of man tumbled
against the stone of ages
the mortar cleft clear by frost
where earth is building
its monument
nudging the rock with a bull's snout of winter
to the blight-brown celebration of weed
rattling their pods

beside the crush of leaning fences
and we crawl up and out
sure handed as a working clock
though we do not mark our own measure
in the tyranny of time.

The Knights of Columbus Lobster Festival, Ancaster

After the feast
we walked to our cars
through mood-swings of late spring
down dark lanes in the dying night
lost in the cave of stars.
And we were full
and content to be ourselves
even the wounded light-torn sky
loved us well in the close cold
and though we walked with strangers
down unfamiliar paths
seeking a gate, a street
a certain tree to guide us by
we were wonderful together
we were amazing
in the soul-stunned beauty
of our own lives
this is what the appetite can do
this is what
can be achieved by food and drink
and fellowship...

yet, when we arrived at the arena
at the noisy centre
of sharp light
brining our gimcrack lobster candles
baskets full of shellfish and crackers
flowing down the length of tables
past the belly-suck of chairs
the room was henna-haired

and chemical coloured
the men balding and only slightly self-conscious.

Meanwhile, we carried our sacks
of sea spiders, three each
our plates drooping like wet hats
our half-cups of cow's gold
melted and going churn-cold
we settled to the business
of solving red shells.
 My thumbs studied the difficult
locks and joints.
First I broke away the quick claw
so mine
became a sinister cull
and then a pistol
"oh, handless creature"
I snapped the tail
and left the amputated carapace
accusing me as a shucked Samurai would
with both black eyes
clicking like costume beads
on a thing half made.
I learned by expert hunger
how to suck the sweet white meat
from the swimmerets
thick like milk-shake straws.
I learned by green tomalley
and red roe to sex the thing

until at last
we sat as in ancient shell circles
our lips butter bruised
our palms slick
and we smiled and drank our health
among what lay
eviscerated in the trash
crabbing backwards
toward the melancholy ocean of the east
sunk into the blue-green danger of the deep

where traps drop doors
on cages
while the wine-cut
washed away the world
with one lovely communal amnesia
of affluence and a common age
we were so middle class
our money almost loved us back.
                    May 26, 1998

The Broken Oak

Dancing through cow flap
gone muddy with age
along the brown and winding Grand
between Paris and home
we come upon a broken oak
hollowed out by time
and high winds cruel to wood.

Oh, to have been present
when it fell on its crooked bones
to have heard it crack
its proof against fools
as with one inquiring weight
it must have crashed
to measure the shuddering ground
more deep
than water shivers after rain.
And we walked the fatal length
from where the trunk
sent up its shell
to where the sky had been disfigured blue
and we found a dozen dry remembers
infolded like younger sweetnotes
clutched and cherished by a dying heart
and each proclaimed
"I'm oak" even when I'm gone,

"I'm oak" and I remember
my own great-great-Auntie in her bed, the cold kiss
that visited the boy I was
and now I know
the young-once nettle of her touch
too late to stay, I know
but in that oak collapsing on its joints
where mayflies once grew dizzy in the dark
I find solace
in a fractured understanding
of the not yet there.

Let Us Stop and Stand a While

Let us stop and stand a while
the trees have things to say.
The pines are whispering snow.
The birches hiss
and God has lain these winter bed sheets
on the hills for us.
See how they sleep
like women's hips beneath the white
while the earth at hand is rolling off
into the valley.
But this is not the moon.

A woman tells me how she lay
as a girl in catalpa shade
suckling her siblings
so they took her nipples in their mouths
like the small box-social kisses
of children
and she, the tree of mothers
strangely thrilled
flowing with the milk of innocence.

A fellow tells me
how he gave the sad white pine
that stood beside his house

a long embrace
then climbed the limbs
then sat there in those uncle's arms
and wept to see the world
because his wife had faded from his life
as if into a grave of fall-green grass.
And so we all are gone under a hollow thump of earth.

Another says
the willow welts the flesh
when mother disapproves
and I see the red lines rise
like pen strokes on her calves
and dogs lie down to die into dreams
where the shade is cool and dark
and the soil is shaved
in dips from sleeping.
So let us stop and stand a while
and see the death-burned elms
the old and seldom-evil oaks
the balm of Gilead of northern Maine
the olive groves of doubt
the eastern deodars
and Douglas firs of the Pacific coast
with Emily's wonder spiraling up to God
among the swirling heavens
of shadow-rippled light.
Stop and drag them through the mind
as they are dragged by winds
combed of death
and cracking like bull boards
of their man-thick limbs.
See how they build their lives
lost between the doll-house logs
of early years
and these ancient autumn leaves
like sweet notes from our youth
unfolding some unremembered, cherished
unsurrendered self
delicate and cracking at the folds.

Roger Bell Is Making Apple Jelly

As you work
I interrupt imagining
a writer's winter appetite
the jelly-lover's pantry
heavy with your own
small summers
the delicate little samples
of what they were
preserved for you
as you set things tight
to damp jam jars
those weird magnifiers
circling sweetness
for that captured season

if we listen
for the apple thud
in the long wizen
of a doll-maker's autumn
or we're ever lost
contemplating the plump creak
of a cider drum
we'll be too late
in that bee-drunk hour
when the frost-dumb wasp
tumbles off the brown-fruit branch
like a fat man's button

no, today's the day
it must be done
let his poems write themselves
in a long grey unthreading of some shadow hand
herein I'll think of Roger's silence
the quiet flavour of his work...as in one delicious pause
the teaspoon's empty sadness
turns on someone else's tongue.

Beer

Because my elder son has come of drinking age
I am thinking of beer.
Because my brother-in-law
is a brewmeister in London
I am thinking of beer.
Because Al Purdy is the poet laureate of beer
I am thinking of beer.
Because I recall
the amber beauty of bell-glass draft
at the smoky York hotel
shining like light on brass
when Cathy sat on my lap
and I felt her innocent and woman warm
that first time
we kissed and then
met the next day
near the shade of the crab
where apples scattered the autumn grass
on the long lawn leading down from learning.
Because of lime in Corona
dark ales and Irish stout.
Because of German bitters
and the slow thick pour of Guinness
at home, where a spoon might stand
as silver sentry
doing duty where the Dublin moon is made of foam.
Because there's memory
of love, of Ernie and us
and afternoons of cards
of Uncle Art avuncular
and easy in a parlour chair
loquacious and liquid
with important talk.
And my friend O'Leary's
gone a ghost so long
I barely hear his absence
though he sings
like a Swansea poet
unchaining the sea link by link for the listening ear.

Because the flavour and shade
of my young life
joins me there
in rivers of barley and lakes of grain
under a golden sun
where I once walked to the waist
in that watery wave of seed
gone to beard.
Because I play hockey
and sit in the sweaty laughter
in the wake of the game
and we share
a cold case
between us taste for taste to remember
and my father
on Saturday nights
of Coca-Cola and popcorn buttered and seasoned with salt
would drink a single squat-bottled Dow
and we'd watch the Leaf's lose.
Because Tom, the hired man
would drink alone at the barn
and leave the empties
under the baler in the shed
where they'd flute the wind
like a wet calliope
and I would never think
her ancient mythic name again
without that mournful music of the mind.
Because cousin George
would stop work
in the sweet tractor fumes of winter
and at his leisure
set the label down
lean in under the low door
inviting us all to rest
and be more human
than we were on the fulcrum of a fork.

Because my elder son has come of drinking age
I am thinking of beer

and not to be drunk or foolish
I think of beer
and float my ever-forgetful heart
on waves of love
like moonlight shining on water while we dream.

A Final Prayer For Allen Ginsberg

Strange now to think of you, gone
                              from Kaddish, Allen Ginsberg

I hold palm up in my hand
your weighty red book
much like a cigar box, really
your Collected Poems
containing wise paper and heavy fire
with the approximate mass
of an old dog's ashes
I open the cover like a lid
but do not find you there, for you were
not just any beard and spectacles
yours was an ancient drum
thumping from the tabla of the human heart
putative godfather of the sixties
sucking your tongue
like a strawberry in the mouth
that old Jew's harp
spittle rich and clucking
to the tom tom-tom of a beatnik's hands
and the jangle of a bright guitar in a smoky club
you were once in Lennon's words
dear old Allen
embarrassing the fuck out of everyone
lying on the floor "ohming"
chanting something called poetry
very loudly
but that particular Beatle's soul
died into the ether
death dumb and ever after, silent

and Timothy Leary, gone as well
with these sweet final words
"sure, why not..." and he expired
with a gentle acquiescence of exhaled joy
as if with a sigh of giggled smoke
he entered the excellent lysergic beauty
of an artist's starry night.
And Ginsberg, you gathered
your friends and lovers at the last
in a circle of eight
and wore yourself out with talking
while the ghost of Kerouac hovered
and the ghost of Hoffman fell
you old pop poet clown
laughing and wearing your jester's lid of glory
while I sat in my room at home as a boy
 thumb-black from reading Rolling Stone.
Meanwhile the wind is howling.
Meanwhile another Whitman
shakes his cloudy hair and whispers welcome
from a singing sky.

Art

According to experts
an octopus
can pour itself
through a hole
the size of its own eye
like liquid licorice
glugging slowly
from a bottle mouth
"at night" the sea world worker says
"it's been known to sneak
through the tubing
between aquariums
to steal a meal"
then slipping home

it bulges
like a floating brain
undulating innocence
a disentangled specimen
of pure thought
hydrocephalic with delight
it sucks the glass
with picture hangers of itself
and dares detection
in the dark this shy fellow leaves behind
an oozing blackness
of happy water
like the hemorrhaging of night
into starless places
he's returning to his cave
an eight leg Casanova
romancing the seven silver sisters
still swimming in his guilty mouth.

Watching Walter Read the Rings of Trees

I am
seeing rain in the rings of felled trees
drought in one circumference thin as a barrel stave
surrounding a summer of fat weather
and there the centuries reside within the wood
the seasons of the willow
the poplar in a decade grew against the eaves
nudging its spear at the seventh shingle
above the mossy spout mouthing heaven
but the slow oak
lifting its shadow branches
to the sad sacrifice of hours
saw a son become a father
in less than the height of a house.
Still, long-toothed saws cut across ages
to ruin over breakfast
what it took ten-thousand hungers to construct.

Shake the nest. Bring tree swings crashing down
with a loose whip of rope
a hanged heaviness
convicting ghosts forgiven by ghosts.
Crack the spoiled shade.
Strew as a storm strews in a snapping damage of beauty.
Take the history of lives
measured in the radius and altitude of elm
and bring it down like green water.
Shake the earth.
See how memory turns to wood.
Make a table of that mystic transformation
with your wedding at your elbow under tea
your birth beneath the heel of your hand
your death, in the emptiness
behind your chair.

On Seeing a Parakeet Among Sparrows

Someone's parakeet is in my yard
where sparrows
sweep up in swarms like drifting smoke
that no one smells
and he's the flash of green
you see
smouldering at the edge
of autumn ash
a fiery feather not quite burned
when the air is brushed with half-extinguished grey
he flames childward
from a faith in fairy's flight
I watch him chased about
an angry sky
halcyon for cages and a kitchen clock
where he might watch
the steam of early evening
steep its whistle on the stove
to fog the glass

or sing against a tiny silver
tintinnabulation of a toy
or groom a single incandescent feather
whispered on the nostril of his beak
the fanned hallucination
some sleeper sees unsatisfied with white
and though he's free
among these peevish perils here
he seems to long
in one exhausted flight
to still the sorrows of the world
and simply light
but paradise it seems
is drab
and all the dramas brown and cruel
stone-fingered statues
lift their purpose
fallen from a sculptor's mind
and pet shops have their own concerns to sing
when doors blow open
to the frantic fancy
of an absent child
meanwhile the sky lifts open
on a line of turning earth
to let an empty darkness down.

An Ingoing

I am here transfixed in a dove's regard
watching
from my flower garden
where she has landed below the blue delphinium
and is going about slow work
in the soft cocoa bean bedding
spiced on a small hill
and she circles
the water mirror of my lily pond seeing herself
walking the mottled
red and grey New England slate

lain there
slate on slate flat as fish scale
in a curved surround
but she cannot solve a difficult thirst
though she sits
a quarter hour before she leaves in rusty flight
to scatter her attention
where jet-trail weather
feathers its fumes
and gone things fade
to an unremembering hue
as though sleeved away by the sweep
of lazy twill
like the chalk ghost of a lesson learned
concerning the rules of light

and where the dove was
in the hen's foot and the foxglove
and the meadow sage and yarrow
and the mock rose
held there   an ingoing of the real
as meanwhile somewhere else
beyond the Chinese elm
and the chestnut redolence
of this particular day
and these shifting brilliant intermingling shades
the dove floats home
in four directions from herself
                    May 11, 1999

In the Terrible Star-Still Night

We were driving through Glencoe
three cousins in a slow car
with *Lay Lady Lay* on the wind
and it was summer
so close the daylight
poured like butter-melt on the glass
as we eased against the curb
our tires rubbed a black chirp

on tramac and gravel smoked up
a snuff of pestle chalk
and there with our windows down
we sat and waited
in the pharmaceutical Sunday
while one girl hitched over
and leaned in
her dark heart beating on the door like a dropped peach
and she said
"Such a nice day out
I think I'll leave it out"
to Stuart at the wheel
who took her innuendo in his mind
as one does testing
the fruit weight of apple branches
with an ache in the small of the foot
and I suddenly knew
we were through
with cock-horse straw brooms
our cap pistols
withering off pretended death
and we'd entered the brand new lethargy
of lazy yearning and doxy ennui
a time of do nothing and say less
like the terrible star-still night.

Adam's Memory

Full born
out of earth
and breath
at the delta of the fourth river
set in the clever clockwork
of his own garden
and lost in the loneliness
of his onomastic task
such things took flight
as if formed from the sparrow flutter

of his naming tongue
though Adam remembered nothing
of himself
until that first sleep of stolen bones
and then from a flood
of inner appetite
became remembering dust
wise darkness
a sentient wind...

how then to know God's meaning
without the presence of the dead
in that ghost-lonely landscape
so pastless and loveless
the dark milk of Adam's memory
has no mother
to grieve
no father to lament
no stones to bless.
When he is gone
the rain
invents a metaphor.

The Chair of Angels
for Brother Paul Quenon

The Shakers
made their brooms
from cornstraw
stalwart enough to sweep
the stars away
and yet
the dew-wet webs
that draped the fences
like beaded purse skeins
stayed their strength
small spiders spun
between white boards

an iron beauty there
to catch the light
that sleepers cannot see
though saved for them
by tiny flaws of mayfly fate
in a crush of ragged wings.

And these Shakers made such chairs
so strong and briefly perfect
that the angels
might alight
upon them, weightless
as the hollow bones of birds.

One time, entire yards
of Seraphim came down
to walk the lawns and watch
while looking out the windows
from their work
the craftsmen
spokeshaved to an awe
so gnurled it fit the dove
like buttermelt
and all the heavens
were a sheet of light...
"come in," they said
"sit down"
and every chair
went brilliant in their hands
and welcome
was a simple breath of wings.
          August 26, 2000

A Certain Grieving

There is a certain grieving that we do
manifest in memory's remembered
and collapsing stone
and as I was standing

under nearby jungle claim
with nature-ruined Chichen Itza
at the mouth of an ancient Mayan well
no longer wet
where you might
count the days by climbing up
to mark the serpent
by its season scale for scale
with the briefly brilliant
and beautiful slither of light
through the span of a single chink
and by heaven's most mathematical
hour—measure life

in solitary solstice
see how we fail immortal longing
in dust shafts of our more corporeal selves
and the priests
            the grand astronomers
            the glory skulls
            and eviscerated virgins
            all the frozen gods
two-thousand-year-old thrills
have settled and are silent here
in this grey rubble
in this archeological puzzle
tumbled to a sacred screed
beneath the slip of certain feet

and every disappearing thing
has whispered to a hush
in the heat of day
on the shade-stained path
the roofless columns stand by temple tens
to truss a weightless blue
mere stars away
with satellites like beetle scuttle
rolling dun planets on their tongues
for all this talk
and nothing but a reverent quiet
to companion poems by

each generation climbing
to the fear
then landing slowly as we step
where we have been
where we have always been.

If I Were But a River Watching

I have seen the river
fatten over the land
wide enough to drown
these low lying houses
and leave
a silt in the hollows
soft as summering
and there
in the thief of flow
our broken boats
that are not boats have come
unfixed and floated away
like startled hen lift
or caught
on the tuft of some
cow-bloat hill
where the meadow smalls
above its shade
or the elm's become
but half itself in the sun
where it is full and upper doubled
in the vanity of its own self-surround
and there, by the crop loss
where sweet corn sank below its measure
and the root-washed beans
spilt down their split sprouts and died
and there
in the fertile afterflood
in the mud-calm
by the creep of green

I see how God
might love us
little by little
how His rivers
might size our doors for shadow
or touch two sides of our pane
to carry the weight of our looking
while we are
mostly looking away.

Crows at Dawn over the Grand Canyon

The sun like greasy water
marks the face of stone with hues of light
and in the canyon
down the red walls, down the orange
and ochre, down the grey, down to where
an absent river
traced its dry arroyos in the dust
like a child's distracted stick
with all the feeble tedium of fever
as if the water knew
its own eventual failure
to reach the sea
and yet it carved
an ancient home
from double voices
and the dizzy climates
where several weathers
mark the altitudes
and all the lazy ages there
the shadows longing to be longer
join their dark and form the night
at some imaginary phantom and eternal hour
and you might have stepped clean
and then mis-stepped into a verge
made deep
and deeper still than you have ever known

dream falling like a weft of web.
And yet the crows of dawn
drop scorch shapes of themselves
like something drifting burning
in the smokeless thermals
of a hovering thought
so impossibly wonderful to be like them
we'd almost run and jump into the vacant thrill
we'd flap our arms
to make the angels form
the way our voices lift and call along the ledges
going into silence
at some distance where we disappear
becoming blue.

Last Night The Starlings

Last night
the starlings
came in visible clouds of early evening
upon a pale blue sky
across the road
above my son and I
who saw them float and form
then fade and go
like shadow scraps
within the looker's eye
and were amazed
as smokes unseen or only briefly seen
where fire fails
or nearly fails in sudden puffs
of heat
combusting something wet
but there they were or almost were
or never were confolding into opaque millions
dark as ink become the lack of ink
translucent as
etiolating haze and thinning

to such clarity of light
as blurs
are solved by bending glass
to find pellucid colours
true within that liquid limpid sand.

And if a whirlwind comes
to lift the dust
it finds a twin
in this the thickening flight
of things
hallucinating weather
where they drift
like tiny time-lapse storms
too brief to photograph.
How suddenly wonderful it is to be alive
to be the resonant bone
which holds huge heaven's small recumbence in a bowl
where event and memory turn and wheel
us curious, uncomprehending and mostly
barely there.
                    —*October 25, 1999*

Night Gone the Shadow of God

When Mark turned grey at eleven o'clock
on the dressing room bench
his skin lamping out
like an autumn salamander
next to a stone in the rain
we knew his distress
and I saw of a sudden
that these were good men
"lie down,"
one said with a knowing concern
"take off your shoes—
are you sick?"
and they gathered around

one rubbing his legs like a lover laughing
a little, one feeling the blue dab of his pulse
for slow sewing
watching his face
for poor maps of the heart
and the room
went round in well-meant jests
as a few of us stood
in the ill
circles of seen light
regarding his fear

"is he dying—I've seen men die
like that...
last year we lost a few"
the ice man says
and he breathes from the sad
deep wells of himself
to recall.

And though we'd played well
yet here we were now
with night gone
the shadow of God
and Mark on the bench
lying down
his eyelids like weeds in the wind
"I can't feel myself," he says
seeing something other than us.
     —November 10, 1999

Walking Along Lake Erie

Some Sundays when my cousins were home
Uncle John would take us
in the truck
down dirt roads
in a trail of amber dust

that floated up and out
like junk-hole smoke let crawl
across the high flat fields
left to scrub thorn
and nettles fallowed by brambles
clarifying to the green crop-wreck of weeds
where poor farmers lived
in clinker-built clapboard time-chafed
on the cliffs above Clearville
and Palmira
and we would walk
where the grass and vines
were espaliered against the bluffs
by the prevailing rain-wasped
breath of God
where the lake had lost its blue
becoming eluant as wash water
and we stepped to where we saw
the scrap of sun-bleached water-dark
driftwood like old-boned men
lying hip and thigh
in the shallow surf
some of it rocking a little
as if locked in the swell and go
of remembered love.

And we gathered fish floats
made into grey-green telescopes to watch
the turn of gulls
we collected the best-pearled shells
to catch the sun glint
and think of something
concerning the inside of ourselves
we came upon and crossed
the muddy privilege of each chill stream
threading its meaning
in a larger thought and being gone
we looked up gullies
and ravines
where spools of fence wire

fell in curled perimeters of measured rust
and old half-chassised automobiles
forgot themselves and found
ferruginous purpose returning to the earth
in slow mustard-coloured rills.
 And we ran and ran
until we stopped, breathing hard
our hearts beating like storm-blind birds
under where the root-nests clung
and the doomed trees leaned
and it was only several hours
once or twice a year
we went sandpipering
to where the autumn ended
and the bent branches
revealed another season
where the thick-hipped cliff
came over-close
and the lake refused us
unwanted as we were in the indolent erosions
of some larger work.

> *February 16, 2000*

Paying Attention
for Mike Wilson

We look down from the hill
and see where the small
and seemingly inconsequential swale
winters below us
and know that it is one of the last precious places
and all along the hogback
we are silent
all down the snow-loud slope
we are wordless
in the slowing of spirit
beneath the beauteous wing span
of God's best creature

riding the waves of heat
above the sun-brilliant meadow
a lone golden eagle
displays its white underwing
working the love of being alive
in the heights
and then
in this landscape
of rough-bark cherry
and larch and the last leaf rattle of low weeds
we come upon the green hallucination
of balsam, a small stand
of colour, and the cedar hush
blind beyond the edges
and know that we are wrong
to ever call the thick dark and deep interior
shadow or shade
it is rather
an artful absence of light
as it is within pure and wordless thought
where we learn the awe
of watching wild turkeys walk
like black scraps in the far valley
and deer grazing the ripe nub of pine
under the bald eagle's flush
and the vulgar profanity of crows.

"Crows love to swear,"
my companion says.
"Hear how they curse that fellow's coming.
 See there, they've set guards above the deer blow
sentinels surrounding
the racket we make breaking trail."
My friend bends down
to show me the fragile downy fronds of ice rim
where the deer track
punched a pre-dawn path
and I see how cold and sunless walking
leaves evidence of its hour

how we might read the thorns
for blood spray
how on the trail of ghosts we seem
and yet in the deep available knowing of nature
it longs to reveal itself and be revered
we simply speak of eagles
and they arrive hovering
above where God is making windows
on the lake.

And I apprehend the truth of wishing
something in the poet-lonely
universe, I realize
the purpose of our being
glimpse it in how this single
solitary man
might save us all
by holding out his hand palm up and open
wherein a swamp secret sits
a single salamander, rare
small, delicate as elderberry pluck.

February 18, 2000

The Last Summer of Canterbury Bells

one summer I remember
how the Canterbury bells bloomed
gas-jets catching flame in Marilyn's garden
and that same year
Ernie was alive
and fishing with spoons
his hook dropping past the still surface
of the water
so the line
hung into the exact centre
of concentric waves
while the red bob throbbed to the deep touch
of sun fish and rock bass

like the last three swivels
of a dying top
and the sweet-corn bait was gone
and the worms
were gone ring by ring
and the table scraps
were ripped away as well
the rags of skin
with their rainbow stains of cooking oil
the small cat bites of roasted hen
and picnic ham
gone, all gone into the weeds
and deep reading
below the surface of the text
where the channel bed
was muddy briefly then clear
and empty
where with your face sinking backwards
into the fallen sky
like a retreating angel
tossing the hook from your mouth
you disappear.

I Would Seduce You

I would seduce you
with the sound of first fruit
dropped in an otherwise empty pail
with the blush
of berries on the bottom
of the box
with the balsa flutter
of a model wing in flight
with the rainbow blink
of bubbles
so close they sting the eye
with colour
in one wet expiring sphere
of startled light

I would seduce you
with the petal pull
of April
breathing from a perfume branch
with a chestnut loss
of blossom
and the burn of snow
I would seduce you
with a tickle rain
that does not touch the earth
beneath the hush of trees
I would seduce you
with a fog
that almost hides the horses
on the Conklin road
I would seduce you
with the float of orchids
kissing their reflection
on my garden pond
where New England slate
is marbled grey and marvelously red
and the foxglove bow
like slips removed
and I would seduce you
with a common love
of water jewels
a brilliant silver kiss
so delicate and strange
it seems extraordinary
theft of breath
and the flexing of a wing enwombed
and fluttering to be born
as butterflies are born
to slow imaginings
of naked sky.

Darling, Where Were You Besides Here

When you feel the human heat
of sitting close in a car
and the mild narcotic of the road
miles you into sleep
and your head rolls against a shoulder
and the light fills up your little space
briefly, then goes out, lonely
like lampfire in the wind
and you dream of breathing
while the radio Beatles you
back and forth in time
so you can't believe
how your father finds his way
without maps
through the three tricky turns he must take
coming home from your grandmother's house
and you wake to the feel
of the night
in the arms of your wife
who strokes your head
and says,
"Darling, where were you
besides here?"

Poetry Books by John B. Lee

Poems Only A Dog Could Love, Applegarth Follies, 1976, PODCL

Love Among the Tombstones, Dogwood Press, 1980, LAT

Fossils of the Twentieth Century, Vesta Publications, 1983, FTC

Hired Hands, Brick Books, 1986 (Runner Up for the People's Poetry Award) HH

Small Worlds, Vesta Publications, 1986, SW

Rediscovered Sheep, Brick Books, 1989, RS

The Bad Philosophy of Good Cows, Black Moss Press, 1989, BPGD

The Pig Dance Dreams, Black Moss Press, 1991 (Winner of the People's Poetry Award) PDD

The Hockey Player Sonnets, Penumbra Press, 1991 HPS

When Shaving Seems Like Suicide, Goose Lane Editions, 1991, SSS

Variations on Herb, Brick Books, 1993 (winner of the People's Poetry Award), VH

The Art of Walking Backwards, Black Moss Press, 1993, AWB

All the Cats Are Gone, Penumbra Press, 1993, ACG

These Are the Days of Dogs and Horses, Black Moss Press, 1994, DDH

The Beatles Landed Laughing in New York, Black Moss Press, 1995, BLLNY

Tongues of the Children, Black Moss Press, 1996 (winner of the Tilden Award for poetry, 1995), TC

Never Hand Me Anything if I Am Walking or Standing, Black Moss Press, 1997, NHMA

Soldier's Heart, Black Moss Press, 1998, SH

Stella's Journey, Black Moss Press, 1999, SJ

Don't Be So Persnickety: The Runaway Sneezing Poems, Songs and Riddles of John B. Lee, Black Moss Press, 2000

Chapbooks and flyers:

Broken Glass, League of Canadian Poets, 1983 (poetry flyer)

To Kill a White Dog, Brick Books, 1982 (chapbook)

The Day Jane Fonda Came to Guelph, Plowman Press, 1989 (chapbook), JF

In a Language with No Word for Horses, Above/ground press, 1997

The Echo of Your Words Has Reached Me, Mekler and Deahl, 1998 (chapbook), EWRY

TABLE OF CONTENTS

I CAN'T BELIEVE IT MYSELF MOST DAYS

PAYING ATTENTION

AGMV Marquis

MEMBER OF SCABRINI MEDIA

Quebec, Canada
2001